THE
VISIONARY

Discover how to turn your vision into a reality.

Learn how to position yourself to achieve success in your visions.

Develop strategies to defeat obstacles to your visions.

FATAI KASALI

Glory Publishing

'The Visionary' copyright © 2021 Fatai Kasali

The author has asserted his right to be identified as the author of this work in accordance with the Copyright, Designs and Patents Act 1988.

All rights reserved. No part of this publication may be reproduced, stored in a retrieval system, or transmitted, in any form or by any means, electronic, mechanical, photocopying, recording or otherwise without the prior permission of the author.

All Scripture quotations, unless otherwise indicated, are taken from the Holy Bible, King James Version, Cambridge University Press, Oxford University Press, Harper Collins, and the Queen's Printers.

Published in the United Kingdom by Glory Publishing

ISBN: 978-1-9996849-7-6

Acknowledgements

To God be the glory for the grace to write this book. I give God all the praise and adoration for inspiring me through His Spirit. This has made possible the writing of this book.

I want to appreciate my family and all those who have contributed one way or another to the beauty of this work. Thank you very much. May God Almighty bless you all.

Introduction

A visionary is a person with the ability to discern and see the future. The eye of his mind is opened to see far and comprehend what ordinary eyes could not detect. A man of vision is a visionary. Without vision, it is impossible to attain greater heights in life. For a better tomorrow, you will need to start preparing for it today. The present situation of your life is a product of how you had lived yesterday, and your tomorrow will also reflect in your today.

The Visionary exposes the meaning of vision and explores the significance of developing vision. You will learn through this book why you need to develop a vision for your life and the attributes required to turn it into reality. Many visions fail because people lack the necessary basic attributes. This book will educate you about what you need to do to achieve your vision.

The mind is always the battlefield, and therefore, if you desire to achieve your vision, you will need to keep your mind sound. You will learn in this book how your mind comes under the attack of the enemy, especially when you are pursuing good plans for your life. You will also discover what to do to keep your mind protected from enemy deception and lies. This book emphasizes the importance of relevant knowledge regarding your vision and the wisdom to correctly apply knowledge to promote it.

Furthermore, if not properly controlled, there are pressures that come against a visionary in the pursuit of their visions which may destroy the visions. You will also learn through this book how to deal effectively with pressures that come with visions.

For the new things to be fully established, the old needs to give way. Therefore, there are vital changes your life will need if you are to achieve your vision. Here, some of such changes and how to adjust your lifestyle to accommodate your new vision into your life situations are exposed.

Life is full of battles, and whenever we aspire to make our lives better, certain obstacles will come in our ways. It is, therefore, important that we are well equipped to deal with such hindrances that want to frustrate our plans. Through this book, you will understand factors that frustrate visions and how to defeat them.

I pray for you that your vision will succeed, and you will remain undefeatable to every negative force that wants to rise against your life in Jesus' name. God bless you.

Contents

Chapter One
Understanding the vision 9

Chapter Two
The importance of vision 25

Chapter Three
The attributes of a visionary 37

Chapter Four
The mind of a visionary 57

Chapter Five
Adjustments for the vision 73

Chapter Six
Knowledge for the vision 83

Chapter Seven
The visionary and the change 99

Chapter Eight
The pressures of a visionary 113

Chapter Nine
Turning vision into a reality 125

Chapter Ten
Psychological warfare 133

Chapter Eleven
The battles of a visionary 143

Chapter Twelve
Enemies of visions 153

Chapter One

Understanding the vision

In the year 2002, by the grace of God, I started the Glory of God Parish of the Redeemed Christian Church of God in the town of Mafeteng in Lesotho, Southern Africa. Majority of the members of this parish were foreigners from different African countries. These immigrants considered living in Lesotho as a stepping-stone to relocate to western countries. Therefore, they were constantly seeking opportunities to relocate to any of the western nations. Unfortunately, these same people were the major donors contributing financially to the operations of the parish. At least, they formed over 95 percent of the financial contributors. The remaining percentage was shared among the local indigenes. About a year after the parish's existence, the Lord asked me a staggering question: *Son, how do you see the future of this parish?*

I answered God: *The future is in your hand, Lord.* Then God proceeded to ask: *What do you consider happening to this parish because majority of members (including you, the parish pastor) are planning to relocate from this country, and you were the major financial donors to the purse of the parish? When all of you relocate, how do you expect the church to survive, considering the financial challenges it is likely to face?*

At this stage, I was short of answers because I did not know how to respond to such likely future challenge the church will face. Then the Lord told me that I should start a nursery school urgently. The idea is that when all the donors leave the church, the Lord will have something He can anoint to be the source of finance to the church. In obedience to this instruction, I started a nursery school in the name of the church. The school opened with just two children from the community. Within three months of its existence, the school grew to the extent that it could finance itself. In 2005, I relocated to the United Kingdom, and a new parish pastor was posted to head the parish. Shortly after my departure from this parish, almost all the major financial donors had left due to relocation to western countries. This drastically reduced the parish's financial strength, but the nursery school generated money that kept the church going. Today, the Lord has blessed the school such that it has grown beyond being a nursery; it now has a primary school. It is the school that is currently financing the church.

Who is a Visionary?

A visionary is a person who can see into the future, see afar, and comprehend matters that are blurry to minds. God wants you to see into the future and prepare for it. The church in Lesotho is still moving forward because of the power of vision.

A vision can be the ability to discern the future. You discern because you could see through the telescope of your mind where you are heading in life. When a man develops a vision for his life, he knows ahead of time who he will become. Vision speaks of what you are going to become tomorrow. The church in Lesotho is financially solid today because yesterday, its future was sorted out through the power of vision. What the church has become today was a product of its yesterday. Vision will help you to sort out your tomorrow through the power of God dwelling inside of you. The most unfortunate thing about life is that whether you have a vision or not, you will become somebody in future but developing a vision allows you to determine who you would like to become in future. A man that has no vision will become what the world shaped him to be, and he will not be able to disagree or reject whatever the world offers him since he has no personal vision for himself.

The exodus of immigrants from the church in Lesotho would have hindered the church's survival, but the church has gone ahead of its future challenges because of the power of vision. Therefore, the church was in good shape to cope with financial difficulties awaiting it when the immigrants relocated from the church. If you can develop a vision for your life, you will put your tomorrow in a better shape to cope adequately with any future challenges awaiting you.

The visionary will not just develop vision but also have visions for different aspects of his life. He will have a vision for his career, family, children, ministry, business, personal development, etc. He will even have a vision for himself when he reaches old age. He will not leave his destiny in the hands of the ever-changing world we live in. He will take personal responsibility for his life and make it better. God wants you to take responsibility for your better tomorrow. When God asked me about what I could see happening to the church in Lesotho after the departure of the financial donors, I threw it back to God, telling God that the future is in His hand. But the Lord made it known to me that I still have a responsibility towards a better future. God expected me to participate in fashioning a better future for His church through His power. Similarly, you cannot throw everything on God as regards your future; you have a responsibility to perform. If you do not care about better tomorrow, God can't impose it on you.

The visionary does not believe in luck but the power of intentionality. He intentionally makes an effort to determine his life situations. Therefore, ahead of time, he knew what his family, career, children, business, etc., would become. His life is not accidental but purpose-driven. He knew what to expect, and he prepares for it. Therefore, his success is never a surprise to him because he knows the effort and purpose he has invested into his future through the power of vision. God instructed me to establish a nursery school for His church as an act of intentionality. That is, a better tomorrow must be intentionally dealt with. A targeted effort must be made towards a better future with specific expectations.

To better understand the meaning of vision, let us examine the subject in different ways.

Vision provides a roadmap to fulfilment. As you grow up in life, you will begin to aspire to become somebody in future. It will be impossible without casting a vision of who you wish to become. Vision gives you a roadmap to walk on, leading you to become the person you wish to become. Therefore, if you will become the person you wish to become, you will need to cast a vision of it and run with it. Vision helps you know where you are going and uncover how to get to the destination. There is a way to every destination, and without vision, it will be difficult to find the way. For example, if your vision for your child is to help him become a medical doctor, when you cast this idea into a vision, you will be able to know the kind of subjects the child needs to do at school and the kind of assistance required.

Isaiah 48:17 (KJV): *"Thus saith the LORD, thy Redeemer, the Holy One of Israel; I am the LORD thy God which teacheth thee to profit, which leadeth thee by the way that thou shouldest go."*

The Bible verse above reveals the intention of God to lead you in the way you should go, but you will need to identify the destination you are going to. When you know who you wish to become, God can then start leading you through the way to follow, for you to become the person you wish to be.

It is, therefore, important that before you begin to search or pray for a way, you will need to first identify the destination that you want to go to. That is the vision.

It is my prayer that as you read this book, the roadmap to success shall be delivered unto you by the Spirit of God in Jesus' name.

Vision is a purpose-driven race. It provides you with a purpose to run for.

1 Corinthians 9:26 (KJV): *"I therefore so run, not as uncertainly; so fight I, not as one that beateth the air..."*

The above Bible verse gives us another implication of vision. It prevents the person from throwing punches at the air instead of the opponent. That is, the visionary acts with an aim. This is because he has identified his goal, and he is pursuing it.

Vision involves setting a goal or target and working towards achieving it. This gets you into a life race with purpose. You constantly have your eyes on a target. It prevents you from a life of distraction. Without vision, there will be no focus.

Proverbs 4:25 says that *"you should let your eyes look right on and let your eyelids look straight before you."* That is, keep your eyes on the target you have set for yourself. That is vision. For example, as a businessman, if you have set a target to double your sales within certain months, this is now a vision to achieve, and you will begin to do appropriate things with this figure in mind. Every change you will be making in your business will be driven towards achieving your target. You will mostly do all things with a purpose you wish to accomplish in your business.

I pray for you that every activity of wasting spirit in your life shall today be cancelled, and as you read this book, you will escape a life of waste without purpose in Jesus' name.

Vision helps you to dictate to life instead of life dictating to you. Life has a plan for you, and unless you have a plan for yourself, you may end up fulfilling the plan that life has for you. The world around you shapes situation around you to make you become what life wants you to become. Personal vision for your life will empower you to dictate to life who you wish to become. When you have a vision, you are better positioned to reject every offer life presents that contradicts your personal vision. When you know who you want to become, you will not allow life to dictate who you should become. In Genesis 39, through Mrs Potiphar, life wanted to make Joseph a fornicator, but the boy refused and stood against the world, maintaining his stand that he was born a leader of nations, not a fornicator. Without visions, a man can conform to whatever life throws at him. A young man was manipulated by his parent to choose a career they wanted him to pursue, but after many years of failure at the university, the boy was eventually allowed to choose the career he personally wanted to study. Without personal vision, you will become what the world wants you to become. I pray that you will receive the grace to resist the pressure life wants to put on you to make you a person contrary to who you wish to become in Jesus' name.

Vision enables you to form a mental picture of tomorrow.

Exodus 3:8 (KJV): *"And I am come down to deliver them out of the hand of the Egyptians, and to bring them up out of that land unto a good land and a large, unto a land flowing with milk and honey; unto the place of the Canaanites, and the Hittites, and the Amorites, and the Perizzites, and the Hivites, and the Jebusites."*

In the story above, God was helping the Israelites to create a mental picture of the Promised Land He plans to give them as an inheritance. God gave them a description of the land so that they can develop accurate imagination of the place in their mental picture. This creates in their mind the nature of the place they were going. This is a vision, for it gives a picture of tomorrow. The visionary has in his imagination the mental picture of his future. He could see how his life will turn out to be after achieving his vision. This enables him not to settle for anything contrary.

Exodus 25:8-9 (KJV): *"And let them make me a sanctuary; that I may dwell among them. According to all that I shew thee, after the pattern of the tabernacle, and the pattern of all the instruments thereof, even so shall ye make it."*

In the above Bible verses, God told Moses that they must make a tabernacle according to the description He has shown them. Do you have the mental picture of your tomorrow? Without a mental picture, you will accept any shape life brings to you. This mental picture will give guidance about choice-making as life brings you different options to choose from.

But without a mental picture, some people's lives have no definite shape—everything is haphazard. This is because there is no description being followed.

Such people marry anybody, do any job, study any course, do any business, earn any salary, live in any area, buy any house, drive any car, befriend anybody, etc. They had no mental image of their tomorrow, and so they accept whatever life offers them. I pray for you that heaven will show you the picture of your future with its detailed description in Jesus' name.

Vision breeds accomplishment. A visionary sets you on a journey of success.

1 Kings 6:14 (KJV): *"So Solomon built the house, and finished it."*

Before Solomon started building a house for God, he had already received detailed information from His father about the house to build for God. That is, before he sets out to build the house, he knew where he was already going. This empowered him not to mess up the project. A man with vision stands a good chance of reaching his destination because he knows what he is doing and where he is going even before starting the journey. Vision gives your life a better shape to function in life.

Where there is no vision, people start a project they will not complete. They start a course they will not finish. People without vision have a lot of uncompleted and abandoned projects in their lives. Therefore, before you begin any project, cast it into a vision. From the initial stage, develop what you want to build and how you want to build it. This is the road to accomplishment. Do not glory that you are building when you do not even know what you are building.

I pray for you that you will always have the desired results in all your works and whatever you start to build, you will finish it in Jesus' name.

Vision creates in you the ability for a positive response to negative circumstances of life.

When a visionary finds himself in a bad situation, he will start working out a way of escape from it. A man of vision easily cast a vision of solution in a mess. He sees opportunity in every wrong situation. For example, if a man of vision finds himself in poverty, he will start exploring how to be rich. If he finds himself in sickness, he will start exploring how to receive healing. If he finds himself in debt, he will start looking for ways to be debt-free. If he finds himself jobless for a long time, he will start exploring the possibility of starting his own business. You can't just sit down crying in your mess. You will need to arise and develop a vision for the way out of your mess.

Nehemiah 1:3-4 (KJV): *"And they said unto me, The remnant that are left of the captivity there in the province are in great affliction and reproach: the wall of Jerusalem also is broken down, and the gates thereof are burned with fire. And it came to pass, when I heard these words, that I sat down and wept, and mourned certain days, and fasted, and prayed before the God of heaven."*

In the above story, people that had no vision came to tell Nehemiah about the terrible situation of the walls of Jerusalem, and Nehemiah developed a vision from it. Nehemiah did not just sit down and join fellow Jews to talk about Jerusalem's situation. He chose to respond positively to the negative situation of Jerusalem. A visionary always responds positively to a negative situation because he will immediately cast a vision of solution to the problem. Every challenge has inside of it a solution that the visionary can only unlock. When you can see beyond the negative situation, you will see opportunities hiding inside the situation.

It is my prayer that as you read this book, the grace to develop a vision to come out of every bad situation of your life shall locate you in Jesus' name.

Vision promotes an effort into better performance. Truly, a man of vision may be doing well, but he still believes he can do better. He will always make efforts to make his life better and better.

Philippians 3:14 (KJV): *"I press toward the mark for the prize of the high calling of God in Christ Jesus."*

In the above Bible verse, Paul says he is pressing towards the high calling. Though at the moment he is doing well in his calling, he believes he can still move higher. He believes he can still do better and better. A visionary is never satisfied with his present achievement level because he always wants to go further and further.

No matter the level of your success, you are meant to keep aspiring for greater success in life. Vision opens the eyes of your understanding not to be satisfied with any level of performance in any area of life. This aids people to catch a vision for better performance in all areas of life.

I pray that you will never stay at one level of achievement, but you will move higher and higher in Jesus' name.

Vision causes a joyful payment of price for the hidden treasure. When a man of vision runs with his vision, he will endure it joyfully; though the journey is painful. The vision makes a man keep smiling in a difficult situation because he sees something good at the end of the journey.

Matthew 13:44 (KJV): *"Again, the kingdom of heaven is like unto treasure hid in a field; the which when a man hath found, he hideth, and for joy thereof goeth and selleth all that he hath, and buyeth that field."*

The future greatness of a visionary is that treasure hid in a field, and nobody could see it except himself. What could make him pay so much price to obtain this hidden treasure is because he sees it and foresees all the benefits it will bring into his life.

As a visionary, the only reason you will not listen to those that will criticise you is that you see what they do not see and thereby ignore their ignorance.

For example, maybe you start spending money to write professional exams, and those who do not see the benefits may start criticising you that you are spending too much money. But if you see the hidden treasure inside, you will not listen to them.

I pray for you that you will not listen to the voice of ignorant people criticising your effort to improving your life.

Vision aspires you to embrace the invisible at the expense of the visible.

A visionary gladly let go of the present (the visible) at the expense of the future (invisible). He runs after the unseen at the expense of the seen.

He is ready to let go of the seen while pursuing the unseen. This is because he has seen something in the unseen.

Hebrews 11:27 (KJV): *"By faith he forsook Egypt, not fearing the wrath of the king: for he endured, as seeing him who is invisible."*

In the story above, Moses chose to forsake Egypt that he could see at the expense of the invisible God. He was able to take such a decision because he could see with his eye of the spirit, a greater honour and reward ahead.

In Luke 5:10-11, James and John left their fishing business to follow Jesus.

The question is: how would they feed their family? Would Jesus give them money? The answer is no.

When a man catches a vision for a certain area of his life, though it is unseen, it will start driving him and controlling visible areas of his life.

For example, a man of vision can resign from his salary job that helps pay bills and start a business that he is unsure when it will start bringing him money. It is the invisible that he saw that is driving him. This act of risk-taking has made many successful people in the world greater than their fellows.

I pray that your spirit man will bring you into greater honour ahead in Jesus' name.

Vision gives you empowerment for change. If you don't want to remain stagnant, develop a vision for progress. If you don't want to stay a failure, develop a vision for success. If you don't want to remain barren, develop a vision for fruitfulness. Vision empowers the visionary to fight for a change. Once your vision enters your spirit man, and you yield your totality to it, it will give you the internal power to face necessary changes that will birth the physical manifestation of your vision.

In 1 Chronicles 4:10, Jabez prayed a prayer of greatness despite being under a curse. In his limitation, he started seeing a vision of greatness. Though being under a curse, he started developing a vision of blessing. He received empowerment to turn his life around. When you are genuinely tired of your present condition, and you develop a vision for a turnaround, there will be an empowerment you will receive that will push you through necessary changes which will lead you to a new life you desired. Proverbs 23:7 says that as a man thinks in his heart, so he will be. That is, it is not the present condition of a man that will determine his future but his thinking. A visionary does not condition his life to his situation. He thinks beyond his present condition and cast a vision for his better tomorrow. This breeds inside of him empowerment to forge ahead and achieve his purpose.

I admonish you to prayerfully develop a vision for a better life, and very soon, you will see God accomplish it in your life.

I pray for you that the grace to see beyond your situation will fall on you in Jesus' name.

Vision gives you the grace to nurture a small thing until it becomes great.

When a man of vision starts a small business, the business will start growing in no time. In the hand of a visionary, small things don't stay small, neither does it die. This is because there is a grace that vision births into the spirit of a visionary. This grace is invisible, but it manifests in the positive development of ideas in the hands of a visionary.

Friend, small things don't just grow bigger except with visions. When you develop a vision, you will be able to work on it and make it bigger.

Zechariah 4:10 (KJV): *"For who hath despised the day of small things? For they shall rejoice, and shall see the plummet in the hand of Zerubbabel with those seven; they are the eyes of the LORD, which run to and fro through the whole earth."*

The above Bible verse admonishes us not to underestimate the little things in the hand of a visionary. This is because a small thing will grow bigger in a short while. There is a potential inside of you that will not manifest until you develop a vision. Many people in our world had surprised themselves. They could not believe that they can nurture small things to become bigger until they see it happen in their lives. There is power behind developing vision. Once you develop a vision and begin to run with it, suddenly, every hidden ability inside of you gets activated into action. There will be a flood of ideas and incredible internal strength that will be released from your spirit man. When you bring your vision to completion, you will look back and discover that you are stronger than you have thought. There is a grace vision brings alive inside the visionary.

I pray for you that the grace to turn small things into greater things shall locate you today in Jesus' name.

Vision causes disengagement from the status quo for a new result.

When a man catches a vision for his life, he will start doing things differently.

For example, if truly your vision is to improve your finances, you will not keep on with the old methods that keep you in debt. You will start exploring a new way of doing things. Vision influences the visionary to try new methods of doing things. It is an exercise of exploration. Visionary gradually disengages from the traditional ways of operation. He will bring in innovation. He will handle new project with new ideas that will work better than the old ones.

In Luke 5:4, Jesus told Peter and the sons of Zebedee to launch into the deep. This is because they have not been able to catch any fish from the side of the water they have been fishing. They will need to try another idea. You can't keep fishing with the same methods that don't work and expect different results. You must launch into the deep, a new arena of water.

People without vision can keep on with old methods that keep on failing. When you are result-driven, you will get impatient using the same old methods that keep failing you. As a visionary who is after better results, you will likely try new ideas and methods.

Jesus Christ gave us a word of wisdom in Matthew 9:17 that we should not put a new wine inside the old wineskin; otherwise, the loss will be great. We should not depend on old methods when we have a new vision. We should be creative enough to explore new methods that will give better and greater results than the old ones. Therefore, whenever you develop a new vision, be ready to explore new methods that can produce quicker and better results. May the courage to try new ideas come on you today in Jesus' name.

Vision creates a path to the attainment of divine destiny.

God has a plan for your life even before He created you. But it is your responsibility to discover the plan of God for your life. Fortunately, God does not leave us to live as an orphan or wanderer. He is constantly shedding His light on our minds so that we can detect His plan and purpose for our lives. It is impossible to discover God's plan for your life without living a life of a visionary. When you become purpose-driven, you will rise to discover God's purpose for your life. You can't grab what you do not chase, neither can you become the person you never dreamt of in your spirit.

Jeremiah 1:5 (KJV): *"Before I formed thee in the belly I knew thee; and before thou camest forth out of the womb I sanctified thee, and I ordained thee a prophet unto the nations."*

The Bible verse above states that God has a plan for your life before you were born.

Hebrews 10:7 (KJV): *"Then said I, Lo, I come (in the volume of the book it is written of me,) to do thy will, O God."*

This revealed that God's plan for your life was written in His book before you were born. It is your responsibility to check out what God has written about you. Unless you are a person with the mind of vision, you will not check out what was written about you before creation.

Philippians 2:13 (KJV): *"For it is God which worketh in you both to will and to do of his good pleasure."*

God is always ready to work in you through His Spirit so that you walk in His purpose for your life. However, a visionary's heart is needed to create a conducive environment within yourself for God's Spirit to be able to work on you. It is the heart for vision that will make you to be vision and purpose-driven. This will make you to always ask God for His plan for every phase of your life. The heart of a visionary will make you ask for God's plan in your marriage so that you don't marry just anybody. Similarly, the heart of a visionary will make you ask God for the career to choose so that you will not study any career. When last do you ask God for His plan for certain areas of your life?

I pray for you that from today, the spirit of a visionary shall rest on you in Jesus' name.

Prayer

- Father, give me the vision of heaven to operate my life in Jesus' name.

- Father, deliver unto me today the heavenly vision for my career, ministry, marriage, finances, education, children, and spouse in Jesus' name.

- Father, by your Spirit, work in me to always will and act according to your good purpose for my life in Jesus' name.

- Father, cause me to always work in your plans for my life in Jesus' name.

- Father, let your light dwell with me always in Jesus' name.

Chapter Two

The importance of vision

The story in chapter one about how the Lord led us to start a nursery school for the church in Lesotho reveals the importance of having a vision for whatever in your hand. God made me see into the church's financial future and instructed me to start a nursery school that He will bless and make to become the financial source for His church so that the church of God will not be forced to close due to financial pressure.

A visionary sees into the future who he will become. God wanted the church in Lesotho to become financially comfortable, so He instructed us to establish a school to generate money to meet the future financial needs of the church. Understanding the importance of a thing will influence the level of significance you will likely place on it. In this chapter, we shall examine the importance of developing a vision for your life with the hope of motivating you to embrace it. You will gain an understanding in this section of how developing vision can influence your life and drive.

Some of the importance of visions include the following.

Proverbs 29:18 (KJV): *"Where there is no vision, the people perish: but he that keepeth the law, happy is he."*

Vision helps people to cast restrain. It brings discipline. A person that has vision will always put himself under discipline to achieve the vision. A student who develops a vision to get a better grade in his examination will notice that for him to improve dramatically in his study, he would need to double his efforts and spend more time in study. This will deny him the opportunity to regularly watch television and reduce the time he will spend playing with friends. Vision enforces self-discipline and brings adjustment to how you live your life as a visionary. Therefore, if your vision is to reduce your debt level, you will need to face the reality that it will require you to adjust your spending rate.

Vision is required for you to possess a possession. That is, for you to possess your possession, it will require that you have a vision.

Genesis 13:14-15 (KJV): *"And the LORD said unto Abram, after that Lot was separated from him, Lift up now thine eyes, and look from the place where thou art northward, and southward, and eastward, and westward: For all the land which thou seest, to thee will I give it, and to thy seed for ever."*

In the above story, God showed Abraham the vision of his possession. God helped Abraham to see it at a far distance so that he can possess it. This implies that you cannot possess what you cannot see with the 'eye of your mind'. It is the development of vision that will open your inner eye to see at a far distance what you dream of possessing.

In **Jeremiah 29:11**, God promised to help you reach your expected end in whatever you put your hands on. This then demands that you have your expected end in mind—what you wish to achieve in your journey. God wants to help you reach your destination, but you will need to see it at a far distance.

Similarly, as a Christian, part of your possession is good health, but you will need to develop a plan or vision for it before it can be yours. For example, to enjoy the good health that God promised you, you may need to be mindful of the food you eat and how you treat your body.

It is part of your possession to enjoy peace, but you will need to have a vision to have peace in all areas of your life, including your marriage, and when you develop a vision for it, you will achieve it very soon. For example, to enjoy the peace God promised you, you may need to ensure that you promote peace in all your dealings with people. Part of your possession is to lend to nations, but you will need to have a vision of how to have in abundance so that you can lend to nations. It is when you develop the vision of abundance that you will be able to achieve it.

Vision helps you to make choices. Life will always throw on your way different things to choose from, but it is the vision that will guide you to the kind of choices to make in life. For example, if your vision is to become an engineer and a university gives you an admission to study medicine while another gives you admission to study engineering; your choice is clear. You will choose engineering.

Hebrews 11:25-27 (KJV): *"Choosing rather to suffer affliction with the people of God, than to enjoy the pleasures of sin for a season; Esteeming the reproach of Christ greater riches than the treasures in Egypt: for he had respect unto the recompence of the reward. By faith* *he forsook Egypt, not fearing the wrath of the king: for he endured, as seeing him who is invisible."*

The story above tells us that Moses chose to suffer instead of a short-time blessing based on the vision of the invincible God he saw. He was passionate about the vision he saw such that he was ready to suffer for it while rejecting the temporary pleasures of sin. What a choice!

What you see will determine what you will choose. When you face so many options in life, your choice will be determined by your vision.

Life experiences taught me that people with visions don't choose just any job or career or marry anybody or live anywhere or have any friends. This is because the visionary will never make choices unless it promotes his vision. People that will add no value to your life have no right to be around you. But it is your responsibility to enforce this.

In Genesis 39, Joseph was imprisoned, but he never chose close associates among fellow prisoners. This was because he knew he was just passing through the prison, and very soon, he would reach his destination. He then chose to wait to get to his destination to choose friends. He did not want to choose friends that will not add any value to his dream and vision. Though he was a slave outside, he never felt like a slave inside. While other prisoners saw Joseph as a fellow prisoner, Joseph saw himself as a future leader, which shaped his choice of associates. Vision dictates choice making.

Therefore, before you make any choice in life, check your vision. Will your choices promote, advance, add beauty, cause fulfilment, or give direction to your vision? If not, cast restrain.

Vision establishes a justification for divine supply. God will not send supply to a person that is not building anything credible.

Resources are a waste in the hand of a man that has no vision. It is the vision that creates justification for God to send you a supply of resources. If you notice that you face constant lack despite all your prayers to God, it could be because there is no evidence that you have any credible vision that could justify the supply of resources by God.

Exodus 36:5 (KJV): *"And they spake unto Moses, saying, The people bring much more than enough for the service of the work, which the LORD commanded to make."*

In the story above, God asked Moses to build a tabernacle for Him, and the same God touched the hearts of people to bring resources for the work. God touched people's hearts to bring resources to Moses because he was building something for God. God is not going to supply resources to you for you to consume and waste. Every resource God gives to His children is tagged to certain needs, such as a need for advancing a vision. Without purpose, abuse is inevitable. Without any target to use, resources for the supply of such resources will likely end up being wasted.

In Nehemiah 1:11, Nehemiah prayed to God to touch the king's heart to show him favour. The justification for that request was based on the fact that Nehemiah was about to build something that will glorify God's name.

It is important to let you know that apart from basic needs for your daily upkeep, any supply from heaven must be tied to something. If you want God to send you a supply beyond your normal general upkeep, there must be something the supply will promote in your life. Such things could be your education, certain project you are doing, career development, etc.

2 Corinthians 9:8 (KJV): *And God is able to make all grace abound toward you; that ye, always having all sufficiency in all things, may abound to every good work.*

The above Bible verse indicates that God will grant you grace to have sufficient supply to promote your good works or your vision that will bring glory to God's name. There must be a certain good work you want to promote in your life before God can send you supply.

It is, therefore, advisable that before you start asking God for abundant supply, the question you should ask yourself is: *abundance for what? What am I going to use the abundance for?*

I pray for you that the grace that will make you qualify for divine supply shall locate you today in Jesus' name.

Vision produces pleasures under pain. When a person is suffering due to the vision that he is pursuing, he will have good reasons to endure the situations. When a man of vision has foreseen the gains that will emerge when he achieves his vision, he will gladly endure all the pains.

2 Corinthians 4:17-18 (KJV): *"For our light affliction, which is but for a moment, worketh for us a far more exceeding and eternal weight of glory; While we look not at the things which are seen, but at the things which are not seen: for the things which are seen are temporal; but the things which are not seen are eternal."*

In the above Bible verse, Apostle Paul reveals that vision made him endure affliction that came his way in the work of God. He even described the affliction as light. To Paul, the affliction is worth enduring. In 2 Timothy 2:10, Paul further stated that he endures all things for the elect's sake. His vision for the Lord's elect comforted him under affliction.

One of the major reasons people quit a plan is due to lack of vision. When you have foreseen the gains awaiting you at the end of the struggle, you would not like to quit. Whenever you see somebody suffering and smiling while pursuing a goal, he must have seen something good at the end of the struggle.

It will be helpful to you to foresee the end gains of whatever you are about to do before you begin. This is because it will comfort you to endure every pain that comes your way. When enemies throw challenges on your way, intending to frustrate you into submission, it will not deter your move because your motivation is based on the aftermath benefits.

I pray for you that the grace to be stronger than your opponents will locate you today in Jesus' name.

Vision promotes the effective use of resources. Where there is a vision, wastage is eliminated. This is because vision creates a channel for the effective use of resources.

Proverbs 29:18 (KJV): *"Where there is no vision, the people perish: but he that keepeth the law, happy is he."*

The above Bible verse has two possible interpretations:

a. Where there is no vision, people waste away.

To perish means to waste away. People with no vision are wasters—they waste away opportunities, resources, precious time, strength, destinies, etc. When you don't have anything productive to invest your time in, you will have time to spend on gossip and unproductive communication. When you don't have a plan for your tomorrow, you will waste away your today. When you don't have a vision for your children, you will waste away the children God gives you. When you establish a business without a vision, you will soon waste away every profit you make from it.

Good things are not all that good in the hands of a visionless man. For example, if you give him a good wife, he will destroy her since he has no vision for her. If you build for him a good house, soon the house will collapse due to lack of care. There are many opportunities lost in the hands of a man that has no vision. A visionless man is a waster. Vision prevents waste. This is because once you have a vision, you can then start channelling all your available resources towards your vision, but where there is no vision, waste is inevitable.

b. Where there is vision, people are effective.

Every opportunity given to a man of vision will be maximised in his hand. He will use it very well. Little resources in his hand will soon become big.

In Nehemiah 2:4, Nehemiah made three requests before the king in response to the king's question. Instead of Nehemiah asking the king for one thing he came for, he ended up asking for three things, and all were granted. He maximised the opportunity presented to him by the king.

This was possible by Nehemiah because before he came before the king, he already had a vision of what he wanted to achieve through the king. He was well prepared to grab every opportunity that could come his way as he stood before the king. Never waste opportunities. Prepare yourself ahead of every encounter and have in mind what you hope to achieve. This will keep your spirit man alert to grab every opportunity that comes your way.

A lady who was a nurse searched for a nursing job but without results. She then decided to apply as a volunteer in a hospital that refused to take her for employment. The lady worked as a volunteer in the hospital with an intention to create an experience in that hospital that can't be ignored. After about six months working as a volunteer, the hospital management noticed this lady's extraordinary performance and decided to give her full-time employment with full payments of all the six months she has worked as a volunteer. This was made possible because the lady envisioned from the onset of her stay in the hospital that by the time she works there for some months, it will be impossible for her dedication and competency to be ignored. With vision, you can increase little opportunity in your hand.

I pray that God will give you the wisdom to operate your life in Jesus' name.

Vision creates room for personal evaluation. Vision creates for you a gauge to measure your life performances. For example, when you know where you are going on a journey, you will know how much distance you have covered and what is left for you to complete. If there is no target you set for yourself to achieve this year, how will you be able to measure your performance at the end of the year?

Until you have a vision, you will never know whether you are doing well in life.

It is your vision that will make you tell yourself that you need to buckle up in life, especially when you compare your present location with how far you still must go to reach your destination.

In 2 Corinthians 3:18, it is stated that we are changing as we behold the glory of the Lord. The glory of the Lord that we focus on becomes our standard of measurement to detect how much we've changed.

Similarly, when you set a vision for yourself, you create a standard for yourself by which you measure your performance as you progress in life. For example, if your goal is to obtain a master's degree and you have just completed your first degree, you will know how much work is left to attain what you desire to become. But where there is no vision, there will be no standard for measurement. Therefore, you will not be able to test if you are doing well in life or not.

Unfortunately, people that have no vision lack any high standard to use for measuring their performance. They will usually compare themselves with themselves. They use their present situation to measure their performance. Such people praise themselves without any form of standard gauge to measure their performance.

2 Corinthians 10:12 (KJV): *"For we dare not make ourselves of the number, or compare ourselves with some that commend themselves: but they measuring themselves by themselves, and comparing themselves among themselves, are not wise."*

Considering the above verse, for instance, a man with a diploma certificate without the vision of furthering his education will always measure himself with his diploma certificate because that is how far he has gone. He may even declare himself a very educated man. This is caused by the limitation of his vision. But when he cast a bigger vision for his education attainment, his comment will change as his vision gets enlarged.

It is wise for you to occasionally pause and evaluate how you are performing in life, considering your life vision. Check how far you have gone and how far you need to go.

May the grace to live a productive life rest on you in Jesus' name.

Vision creates a path to a fulfilled life. A person that lives a fulfilled life is the person who achieved what God created him to achieve in life. There is a reason why God created you in this world. To fulfil the purpose of why God created you, you need to be a visionary—a man that runs his life with the future in mind.

2 Timothy 4:6-7 (KJV): *"For I am now ready to be offered, and the time of my departure is at hand. I have fought a good fight, I have finished my course, I have kept the faith."*

Paul looked back, and he said he had fulfilled his purpose on earth; therefore, he was ready to die. How did he know that he has fulfilled his purpose of existence?

Acts 26:19 (KJV): *"Whereupon, o king Agrippa, I was not disobedient unto the heavenly vision."*

Paul received a vision from heaven about his reason for existence, and he ran his life with it.

1 Corinthians 9:26 (KJV): *"I therefore so run, not as uncertainly; so fight I, not as one that beateth the air:"*

The above explains that what Paul saw in a vision controlled his life.

You need to know that God has a plan for every area of your life, including your marriage, career, job, ministry, business, etc. As God reveals His purpose for various segments of your life, it will be your responsibility to apply it to yourself.

When you catch the revelation of your children's future, career, ministry, business, etc., and start running your life with it, at the end of your days, you also will look back and confidently speak that you have been fulfilled in life.

May you live a fulfilled life in Jesus' name.

Prayer

- Father, show me the vision of heaven concerning my career, ministry, marriage, education, business, etc., in Jesus' name.
- Father, the grace to obey the vision of heaven concerning my life, let it locate me today in Jesus' name.
- Father, remove distraction from my ways in Jesus' name.
- Father, let all my visions speak in Jesus' name.
- Father, help me to dwell constantly under an open heaven in Jesus' name.

The Visionary

CHAPTER THREE

The attributes of a visionary

A visionary is a person that sees into the future. Vision is about what you see yourself becoming in future.

You may need to ask yourself: what do I see my career becoming in future? What do I see my spouse becoming in future? What do I see my children becoming in future? What do I see my ministry becoming in future? What do I see my business becoming in future?

If you look at the various aspects of your life as they appear presently, what appearance do you expect them to transform to in future? If you forecast a negative outcome, then you may need to develop a vision based on what you expect them to become in future.

For you to be able to intentionally determine the future shape of various areas of your life, you will need certain attributes. Life is about skills. Though you may have a good interest in making your future better, the interest will only stay in your heart and not in your hand without the necessary skills.

Let us examine basic attributes you will need for you to develop and pursue visions for your life.

1. Ability to start small.

To have a better and great future will require that you be wise and courageous enough to start small. To start small implies that you start pursuing your visions with little resources in your hand. Do not wait until you have great resources before you start making efforts to make your tomorrow better. The achievers that have great things today will tell you that they started small and advanced little by little until the small things of yesterday became great in their hands.

In His word, God wants you to start small.

Zechariah 4:10 (KJV): *"For who hath despised the day of small things? for they shall rejoice, and shall see the plummet in the hand of Zerubbabel with those seven; they are the eyes of the LORD, which run to and fro through the whole earth."*

Job 8:7 (KJV): *"Though thy beginning was small, yet thy latter end should greatly increase."*

The two Bible verses reveal that though you start small, things will not remain small. God expects you to start building your better tomorrow with the little resources in your hands. Never wait for the time that you will have all the needed resources for building a better tomorrow because such moments may never come.

Why does God want you to start your vision small?

a. God wants to help you develop your faith as He takes you from stage to stage in your vision.

We grow in faith when we start big things small as we see God lifting us up gradually through various situations on the way.

The journey from small things to great things will expose you to various challenges that will require your faith to overcome them. As you overcome those challenges on the way, your faith will keep growing to trust God for greater things in future. God wants to help you build stronger faith for the days ahead and starting small is one of the avenues to achieving it.

b. God wants to help you develop a testimony of your achievement/success.

Starting small will make you have a testimony of how God has helped you through various challenges on the way. This testimony will encourage somebody tomorrow. People will hear your testimonies of success and start trusting God for their own achievement, believing that if God can do it for you, He will also do it for them. In your success, God wants to help other people to achieve success through your testimony of God's faithfulness.

c. God wants to help you identify those who genuinely believe in you.

Everybody would like to be part of big things, but very few would like to be part of small things except those who believe in you. When you start small, only those who believe in you will join you to build a better future for yourself. Those who do not believe in you will step aside because they don't see a future in the small thing in your hand. This will help you to know those to trust and not to trust. Starting a big thing in a big way will open you to deception, believing that all those who join you believe in you.

Some years ago, we wanted to start a branch of our church, and we invited an elderly Christian brother for counsel and support, but he refused to offer any help. This brother even discouraged us by sowing the seed of unbelief in our hearts, but the grace of God upon our lives gave us victory.

A few years later, when the church grew, this Christian brother started saying that we started it together.

Everybody wants to be part of big things, but very few would like to be part of small things. Only those that genuinely believe in you will join you in building with small things. God wants you to start small to help you so that you will not depend on the wrong people.

God provided those little resources in your hands to help you start small, and as you progress, He will release more resources to you.

I pray for you that the grace to enlarge small things to big things will locate you in Jesus' name.

2. Be a multiplier.

One of the attributes you will need to achieve your vision is to be a multiplier.

Who is a Multiplier?

a. A multiplier is a person that can use one to take over many.

John 4:7 (KJV): *"There cometh a woman of Samaria to draw water: Jesus saith unto her, Give me to drink."*

In the above Bible verse, Jesus Christ entered the city of the Samaritans, and He encountered a single woman from the city. At the end of the conversation, the woman believed in Jesus Christ and then went into the city to announce to fellow Samaritans.

John 4:39 (KJV): *"And many of the Samaritans of that city believed on him for the saying of the woman, which testified, He told me all that ever I did."*

The above scenario shows that other Samaritans that came through the testimony of the single Samaritan woman believed in Jesus Christ.

This story reveals that Jesus worked through a single woman to capture the whole city. It is very clear that from the onset, when Jesus started having an encounter with this woman, He already had in mind to capture the whole city. That is, Jesus had a purpose to achieve through this woman. His vision was to capture the whole city through this single woman. He used one to take over many.

This same strategy used by Jesus can be applied to your life. For example, suppose you have a business whereby you deal with members of the public, you can intentionally use one to take over many through the way and manner you deal with every single customer that comes to patronize your business. You must intentionally determine that you will offer good services to every customer that comes to your business such that they will have an experience that will make them introduce your business to friends and relatives. From one customer, you will begin to attract many. When you find a businessperson, who runs his or her business with a vision of having more customers in the future, he or she will render great services to every customer who patronizes his or her business with the hope that they will bring more customers in future.

b. A multiplier is a person who can make gains.

Matthew 25:14-15 (KJV): *"For the kingdom of heaven is as a man travelling into a far country, who called his own servants, and delivered unto them his goods. And unto one he gave five talents, to another two, and to another one; to every man according to his several ability; and straightway took his journey."*

In the above Bible story, a master gave talents to his servants, but he did not tell them what to do with them. He wanted to test their mind.

The story later reveals that those with the mind of increase traded with their talents and made an increase, but the one without the mind of increase buried his own.

A multiplier is a person that can make gains with whatever committed into his or her hand. God does not want little thing to remain little in your hand. He wants you to constantly be thinking about increase. Even when God gives you a little opportunity in a place, He expects you to work on that opportunity such that it will increase. As you do better with one opportunity committed into your hand, more opportunities will then be committed into your hand. Those who favour you can grant you more favour if they are impressed with how you handled the first favour you were given.

I pray for you that the anointing to multiply blessings shall come on you today in Jesus' name.

3. Be a penetrator.

A penetrator is a person who can force his way through a thing. When you come across an obstacle on the way, you should not be too quick to quit but to force your way through. There is a general saying that the bigger the vision, the bigger the challenges to overcome. This is generally true about greater pursuit. Therefore, you should get yourself ready to give a fight to any form of obstacle that may want to stand in your way.

Let us examine a penetrator in two ways:

→ A penetrator is a wall breaker.

He can break through a wall of hindrances.

Mark 5:25-27 tells us the story of a woman with the issue of blood that came to see Jesus for her healing, but unfortunately, she was prevented from seeing Jesus due to a large crowd that gathered around Jesus. This woman was then faced with two options: either to return home and try next time or devise a means to overcome the obstacle. The woman chose not to return home with her sickness but to overcome the obstacle. She penetrated through the wall of the crowd, touched Jesus' garment, and obtained her healing. She was a penetrator. But the story earlier reveals that before the woman came to Jesus, she already had a vision of seeing herself being healed of her infirmity. When she came across the obstacle, her vision strengthens her to defeat the obstacle. People who genuinely have visions do not easily surrender to obstacles but receive strength from their desire to defeat the obstacle.

A penetrator breaks through any wall of obstacle standing in the way of his or her vision.

There is strength in vision. Vision induces strength to those that possess it.

People that lack vision easily surrender to hindrances and start giving a catalogue of excuses. When you refuse to surrender to obstacles, your inner strength will rise within you, but if you feel defeated in the face of obstacles, the inner strength will become passive.

→ **A penetrator is a ceiling remover.**

Ceiling is a limitation set over the life of a person by both internal and external forces. When you accept the ceiling set over your life, you will not see yourself rising above the limitation of life. Furthermore, this ceiling could manifest in the form of life turning you back, telling you that there is no space for you. Life can tell you that you are not fit to be accepted into certain positions, but if you refuse to consent, you will be able to remove the ceiling and create space for yourself.

In Mark 2:3-5, four people brought a man sick of the palsy to Jesus, and when they could not find a space to come before Him, those people then uncovered the roof, broke it up, and let down the bed wherein the sick of the palsy lay. These people are penetrator, able to remove the ceiling that denied them space before Jesus.

When life tells you that there is no space, do not concur but put on a fight to remove the ceiling to create space for yourself.

Sometimes, life will tell you that there is no space for you, but there will soon be space available if you can hold onto your dream and vision. Vision compels people to have space for you and accommodate you.

In Genesis 40, the world put Joseph in prison because they had no space for him and his dream, but the man held on to his dream. Shortly after that, the King of Egypt created a space for Joseph on top. His dream of many years came to fulfilment.

Many successful people known in the world today were unknown yesterday because the world told them there was no space for them, but the same world created space for them because they held on to their dream and vision.

I pray for you that the anointing that creates space on top shall work for you in Jesus' name. I also pray that every limitation built around your life shall be removed today in Jesus' name. May the world have space to accommodate you and your vision in Jesus' name.

4. Be a carrier of the light of vision.

Acts 9:3 (KJV): *"And as he journeyed, he came near Damascus: and suddenly there shined round about him a light from heaven:"*

Vision and light work together. Wherever you see a vision, there is always light—a spiritual light.

Once you genuinely develop a vision for your life, light is switched on to lighten your path.

What is the purpose of this light?

a. The light of vision enables you to identify your destiny helpers—those God has sent to you to help you fulfil your destiny.

1 Chronicles 12:22 (KJV): *"For at that time day by day there came to David to help him, until it was a great host, like the host of God."*

In the story above, God started sending destiny helpers to David to help him to become the person God created him to be. The anointing of God upon David enabled him to identify those helpers God sent. He welcomed them into his camp, and they helped him to be fulfilled in life.

When you develop a vision, a spiritual light is switched on within your spirit man to lighten your path. This light helps you to identify those that have come to aid your vision. Your instinct will always tell you if those that have come to work with you are for you or against you. In Genesis 40:12-17, Joseph met a man in the prison, and he interpreted his dream to him. But at the end of their encounter, Joseph told the man to please introduce him to the king for help. The light of vision inside Joseph enabled him to identify the man as a destiny helper, able to advance his fulfilment. The story later turned out that Joseph was right because the man eventually introduced him to the king.

If you have a vision, your eyes of understanding should be opened to see the hidden details that could affect your vision.

b. The light of vision also enables you to identify those that God has not sent to you.

The devil probably sent them to destroy your vision.

2 Samuel 3:21 (KJV): *"And Abner said unto David, I will arise and go, and will gather all Israel unto my lord the king, that they may* *make a league with thee, and that thou mayest reign over all that thine heart desireth. And David sent Abner away; and he went in peace."*

In the story above, Abner came to David, promising him that he will make Israel choose him as king, but David did not welcome him. David sensed that God did not send him to help his destiny. The light of vision that was inside David gave him access to the hidden details as regards Abner.

A man that has no light of vision welcomes anybody seeking human help into his life. When Devil sees that you are a vision/purpose-driven person, he will make series of attempt to complicate your purpose by sending wolves in human skin to you, who will pretend as helpers. But the light you've received when you developed your visions will enable you to identify them.

I pray for you that God's light will continually shine on your path in Jesus' name.

5. Have the end in mind.

To have the end in mind means that you are controlled by the outcome of your vision. You are not controlled by the present but the result. You could see what you are becoming as you pursue your dream.

If you will achieve your vision, you mustn't be moved by the changing prevailing situations but the outcome. Your attitude and reaction to situations along the journey must be determined by the result you aim to attain. Therefore, while you start small, begin to speak big because the end will be bigger than the beginning. When you think about how situations are developing, think big because the end will become bigger than the beginning. When you plan, let it be big because the end shall be bigger than the present prevailing situations. Do not be carried away by present situations which may appear ugly but focus on the beauty that will emerge at the end of your struggle.

God wants you to have the end in mind to keep your motivation on. God is more interested in who you will become rather than who you are. That is why God will always address you based on who you are becoming rather than who you are.

Romans 4:17 (KJV): *"(As it is written, I have made thee a father of many nations,) before him whom he believed, even God, who quickeneth the dead, and calleth those things which be not as though they were."*

God calls things that are not as if they were. He spoke to Abraham with references to what He saw him becoming, not who he was at that moment. While Abraham was still barren, God described him as a father of many nations. God was more interested in who he would become, not who Abraham was at that moment.

God would not speak about the present because it was a passing phase. Similarly, you must treat your present as a passing phase of your life while you constantly welcome your emerging future, which is bigger than your present.

Why is it important for you to have the end in mind?

It is to prepare yourself for the coming success when your visions materialise. Many people were caught unprepared for greatness because they never saw it coming to them—so they could not prepare for it. When you prepare yourself for an approaching greatness, you will not miss every opportunity that will come your way to advance your vision. An unprepared mind cannot see into the future because it has absented itself from it through lack of preparation. When you have the end in mind, you will hook yourself to the end while you free yourself from the present. Having the end in mind enables you to gradually free yourself from the present prevailing situation while gradually attaching yourself to the incoming greater success.

When you have the end in mind, you don't live to adapt to your present situation, but you will get yourself ready for the great thing coming. When you have the end in mind, you don't evaluate yourself based on your present situation but your future situation. What you have seen yourself becoming will be more important to you than what you are at present. Even those mocking you based on your present situation will not attract your attention because you know your real self will soon emerge in the future, which will shut the mouth of every mocker.

I pray for you that God's hand will move you from glory to glory in Jesus' name.

6. He can handle momentum.

A person of vision should be able to handle momentum if his vision comes to pass.

Momentum is the force in motion. Vision and motion go together because vision sets you in motion. You can't have visions and remain stationary or passive. A man of vision is always on the move, chasing and running after his vision.

There are three things you should know about momentum when it comes to visions:

→ A man of vision can generate momentum.

He can cause revolution, changes, and movement to advance his vision. He is a mover.

Acts 17:6 (KJV): *"...these that have turned the world upside down are come hither also."*

The people used the above Bible verse to describe disciples that have turned the world upside down. The vision pursued by the disciples had consumed them such that they became movers, moving the whole city and creating impacts that could not be ignored. They set things in motion as they pursued the vision God gave them. Their action generated noises and revolution. They caused a lot of shaking in town.

You need to understand that it is never quiet with a man that has vision because he is always doing something to promote his vision, and when he acts, it is noticeable.

Furthermore, vision does not only sets you in motion, but it also does the same to people around you. You can't have a vision without passion because when you develop vision, it becomes your passion. This passion will grow such that even people around you will notice it. It is like a young lady who just falls in love with a man she has been praying for. Her look will radiate joy such that those around her will notice something interesting is happening in her life. Such a lady will defend her new lover and speak well of him, and she will influence people around her to embrace her new lover.

1 Corinthians 9:26 (KJV): *"I therefore so run, not as uncertainly; so fight I, not as one that beateth the air."*

The above Bible verse was written by Apostle Paul. He revealed that he ran with a vision in mind. His vision generated within him momentum. It sets him in motion. Certainly, when Paul ran, those that worked with him will also run. That is the impact of vision.

Are you passionate about anything? If not, it is likely that you have no vision. If yes, I congratulate you, but please, keep running with your vision. Keep yourself in motion. Keep chasing your vision. Keep moving things around in your life in the direction of your vision. Keep spending your resources in the direction of your vision. Keep directing your energy in the direction of your vision. Keep seeking helpers in the direction of your vision. Keep getting people around you involved in the direction of your vision. Let the world see that you are married to your vision.

I pray that before this year ends, the world will celebrate you in Jesus' name.

→ A man of vision can catch momentum.

Vision keeps you on alert to grab every opportunity that comes around you that can promote your vision.

Ecclesiastes 9:11 states that the race is not to the swift, nor the battle to the strong, neither yet bread to the wise, nor yet riches to men of understanding, nor yet favour to men of skill; but time and chance happeneth to them all.

This implies that it is God that creates time and chances. God determines the time when certain opportunities will come your way. God expects that your vision should get you ready always such that whenever the opportunities come on your way, you can grab them. For you to be able to catch momentum means that when God moves favourable events in your direction, you are available to take advantage of them. You don't miss your opportunities.

Ecclesiastes 2:14 (KJV): *"The wise man's eyes are in his head; but the fool walketh in darkness: and I myself perceived also that one event happeneth to them all."*

To have your eyes in your head implies that you are alert and sensitive enough to take advantage of every opportunity. Your

The attributes of a visionary

vision is supposed to keep you awake in the spirit of hunting for every opportunity that can promote your vision. God wants your vision to succeed, but as He opens the door of opportunities for you to advance your vision, you should be clever enough to grab them. When God wants to generate momentum for you, He causes shaking for your sake. He can move things around for your favour.

For example, for your sake, God may create a market for your products to be advertised, or He may set up a stage for you to dance so that people that matter can notice your potential.

Therefore, whenever you notice certain shaking around you, it could be that God is generating momentum for you. Your responsibility is to just catch the momentum and don't let it slip from your hand.

In 1 Samuel 17, David noticed a moving force in town. He heard about the fear and bragging of Goliath. David's spirit sensed that this noise about Goliath was for him, and he caught the momentum and stood against Goliath in the battle of supremacy. He won, and from that moment, he started moving from glory to glory.

When challenges come knocking at your door, it could be that God is creating an avenue for you to advance your vision because inside every challenge is an opportunity to step up to another level.

I pray for you that whenever God create momentum for you, you will be available to take advantage of them in Jesus' name.

→ A man of vision can sustain momentum.

A man of vision will not only shine, but he will keep on shinning. He will not only reign, but he will keep reigning. This is because he moves from vision to vision. As he is finishing one vision, he is starting another one. As such a person is causing shaking now; very soon, he will cause another shaking.

Proverbs 4:18 states the path of the just shines more and more unto the perfect day. That is, the righteous man shall keep doing great things. He sustains successful accomplishments.

Daniel 6:28 reveals that Daniel prospered in the reign of Darius and the reign of Cyrus the Persian. Daniel sustained dominion; he reigned from kingdom to kingdom. He sustained momentum. The opportunities to reign that God gave Daniel never diminished or slipped out of his hand. When Daniel caught the vision of being spotless before God, he became great in a foreign land, and he sustained it such that even when a new king came to power, he retained Daniel in his prosperous position. He sustained the momentum God created for him. Important personalities become people of yesterday because they could not sustain momentum. They could not sustain themselves in the position of privileges God established for them.

I pray for you that in all your days, you will never be an ex-champion in Jesus' name. I pray that your promotion shall endure time, your joy shall endure time, and that the anointing of God upon your life shall endure time and multiply in Jesus' name.

7. He is not a quitter.

A quitter is a person that lacks enough courage to face opposition and thereby gives up his purpose. If you want to be a visionary, get ready for challenges. History has shown that every successful attempt has records of once overcoming obstacles. It is not common that a great idea will come into fruitfulness without any major hindrance.

Philippians 3:14 (KJV): *"I press toward the mark for the prize of the high calling of God in Christ Jesus."*

Paul made the above statement during the time he was facing challenges during his ministry. Instead of stopping the good work, he pressed on against opposition and hindrances. If you don't want to quit your vision, you must learn how to press on against all odds coming against your plan. You must resist every resistance coming against your plan. You must fight whatever is coming against your plan. You must be determined to reach the finish line of your vision.

The Book of Hebrews 12:2 advises that you must keep your focus on Jesus.

Hebrews 12:2 (KJV): *"Looking unto Jesus the author and finisher of our faith; who for the joy that was set before him endured the cross, despising the shame, and is set down at the right hand of the throne of God."*

If you keep focusing on challenges instead of Jesus, the pressure of challenges may deceive you to quit your good idea. Whatever you focus on will appear bigger than its normal size. If you keep focusing on Jesus, God will appear bigger than your challenges. But if you keep focusing on your challenges, your challenges will keep appearing bigger than their normal sizes. This will overwhelm you, and it will drain your faith. The consequence will be dropping out of the way.

The impact of weariness can result in quitting. Therefore, when you notice that you are getting weary of the situation, relaxation may be necessary; otherwise, exhaustion may take you out of your good plans.

Galatians 6:9 (KJV): *"And let us not be weary in well doing: for in due season we shall reap, if we faint not."*

THE VISIONARY

This verse advises that you must not surrender to weariness. For you not to surrender to weariness will require that you relax or seek divine support. People quit good plan because they get tired of the situation. Their effort is not yielding the expected result, and they become weary of the situation. It is important to state that sometimes, weariness could be due to carrying excess loads than you can bear. In that situation, you may need to shed some. You can seek helpers to assist you in your vision instead of carrying the whole load of responsibility. In your drive to attain your vision, understand yourself in terms of the limitation of your ability. Do not drag yourself beyond the limit; otherwise, the pressure may come on you and drag you out of the way.

Furthermore, when situations become dragging and slow, the deception to quit may grow within you, but you must be determined not to quit because things are not moving speedily as you have imagined. In circumstances that situations are not progressing as you've envisaged, be patient and do not quit. Sometimes, it is better to permit the situation to pass through its natural stages for a better result.

Irrespective of what happens, never accept that your vision is not possible.

Do not allow series of contradictory events that may come your way to convince you that your vision is no longer possible. Remember that you can never defeat any challenge by running away from it. You must confront it strongly. The pressure of challenges demands that you keep increasing in strength. As you pursue your vision, keep increasing in knowledge, wisdom, tenacity, faith, hope, expectation, and every virtue that will enable you to combat any increase in challenges. Always update yourself as you advance with your vision. The solution to not giving up is to partner with God. Let God be your strength in your pursuit. With God, nothing shall be impossible.

Prayer

- Father, make me a person of open eyes; help me see what you want me to see. When you open doors of opportunities for me, let me see it, and when you generate momentum for me, let me notice it. Oh Lord, help me not to miss my time.
- Father, let all my visions succeed greatly in Jesus' name.
- Father, finance all my visions and supply me with all the resources needed for my vision to manifest in Jesus' name.
- Father, uphold me by your right hand as I pursue my vision in Jesus' name.
- Father, strengthen me by your Spirit and make me stronger than any obstacle that wants to stand against my vision in Jesus' name.

Chapter Four

The mind of a visionary

A visionary is a person that sees into the future and identifies who he or she is becoming. It is important to state that how far you will go in whatever you put your hand on is determined by the state of your mind. This is because it is your mind that you'll use to assess the situation and make decisions about the line of action to take. Therefore, the state of your mind as regards your vision will determine the outcome of your vision.

As a visionary, you need certain types of mind if your vision will come to fruition. In this chapter, we shall examine the types of mind your vision will need so that you can make an intentional effort to develop your mind in that direction.

1. Enlightened mind

This is a mind that has been trained as regards the vision. It is important that before you embark on your vision, you need to enlighten your mind about it. You will need to educate your mind about all the necessary knowledge related to your vision.

A mind that lacks knowledge will mess up vision no matter how good it appears.

Acts 7:22 (KJV): *"And Moses was learned in all the wisdom of the Egyptians, and was mighty in words and in deeds."*

The above Bible verse reveals that before Moses started his ministry of taking Israel out of Egypt, he first learnt about Egyptians. He learnt their culture, tradition, language, mentality, and ways of life. This exposure gave him understanding and knowledge about the vision he was about to pursue.

Exodus 26:30 (KJV): *"And thou shalt rear up the tabernacle according to the fashion thereof which was shewed thee in the mount."*

Similarly, before Moses started building the tabernacles, he was taught by God about what he was to build. He knew what he was about to build before he started building. He enlightened his mind.

Numbers 13:17-18 (KJV): *"and Moses sent them to spy out the land of Canaan, and said unto them, get you up this way southward, and go up into the mountain: and see the land, what it is; and the people that dwelleth therein, whether they be strong or weak, few or many."*

In the same vein, before Moses and the army of Israel invaded the land of Canaan, they first gathered information about the land. Moses mind was trained to get enlightened about whatever he wanted to pursue. He always acted under relevant knowledge.

Visionaries don't embark on any vision without first gathering relevant knowledge about the vision. If you want to succeed in any vision, you will need to train your mind regarding that vision.

For example, if your vision is to become an engineer, you will need to seek the knowledge relevant to engineering to help you make a good decision along the journey.

If your vision is to produce children that fear God and useful to Him, you will need to educate yourself about what it means to fear God and be useful to God. Before you choose to become anything in life, you need to seek relevant knowledge about it. It is impossible to become what you don't know.

Proverbs 19:2 (KJV): *"Also, that the soul be without knowledge, it is not good; and he that hasteth with his feet sinneth."*

Your mind is part of your soul. An untrained and unenlightened mind will act and think in darkness. Before you start any project, train your mind and get understanding so that you know what you are entering. This will improve the way you will think as you face different situations. Without proper enlightenment, your mind will lack the capacity to think rightly. Wrong decisions will be imminent without proper knowledge. Waste of useful resources will be unavoidable when the mind is in darkness.

Never enter an unknown territory without first educating yourself about it.

I pray that the light of God be shed upon your mind in Jesus' name.

2. A wise mind

This is a mind that has the wisdom to handle the vision. Wisdom is the application of knowledge. Unfortunately, not everyone that has knowledge is able to apply it. This is because no matter how knowledgeable you may be, there will still be something you do not know. Therefore, you need to pray to God for the spirit of wisdom.

1 Kings 3:9 (KJV): *"Give therefore thy servant an understanding heart to judge thy people, that I may discern between good and bad: for who is able to judge this thy so great a people?"*

When Solomon took over the leadership of Israel from David, his father, he investigated the task ahead of him and identified that he would need supernatural infilling of wisdom. He approached God to give him a wise mind.

Why do you need a wise mind for vision?

- **For appropriate application of knowledge.** Some people have knowledge but apply it wrongly. If you have supernatural infilling of wisdom, you will be able to apply whatever knowledge you have about your vision rightly.

- **To judge situations.** Sometimes, the line of demarcation between good and evil can be very thin. Even good and bad people may appear similar before you, but wisdom will help you identify good and evil. Many good vision has been destroyed because somebody rejected good and accepted evil out of error because he did not know. Some people send helpers away and accept destroyer into their vision out of error. You need wisdom to judge the situation clearly and identify any thin line of demarcation between good and evil.

- **To make choices.** Without sound wisdom, making choices will become a challenge. As you pursue your vision, situations may present before you many options, and you will need to choose. It is wisdom that will help you choose rightly among many options.

- **To identify open doors.** This is in terms of opportunities that may advance your vision. You will need wisdom to identify some strange and hidden opportunities that will be coming your way. Sometimes, God opens a door for you to advance your vision, but it may not appear visible, but wisdom will help you identify such doors of opportunity. Many visions had collapsed because people concerned could not identify opportunities that would have promoted their visions. Such people keep on missing opportunities.

- **To see beyond the present.** Wisdom helps you see into the future and position you to make decisions based not only on the present but the future.

Isaiah 11:3 (KJV): *"And shall make him of quick understanding in the fear of the lord: and he shall not judge after the sight of his eyes, neither reprove after the hearing of his ears."*

The Bible verse above shows that there are two types of sights:

1. Insight—which you use to see the invisible part of a situation; and
2. Outsight—which you use to see the visible part of a situation.

Similarly, in every situation, there are two parts: the visible part, which is about the present condition of the situation, and there is the invisible part, which is the future condition of the situation. The visible part is open to everybody, but only those with insight can see the invisible part—which matters most.

It is wisdom that can help a man to see a bright future in a dire situation despite the prevailing ugly present condition. It is wisdom that gives a man insight into seeing the invisible part of a situation and making wise choices. Those people who have insight don't make choices based on what could be seen visibly but unseen.

For your vision to be fulfilled, you will need insight and the ability to see what is not visible about your situation and make decisions based on it. For your vision to succeed, you need insight more than outsight.

I pray for you that you will receive a heart of wisdom to always make wise decisions in Jesus' name.

3. Authentic mind.

This is a mind that is original, and whatever it does is not copied from any source. Its decision is not a product of external but internal factor.

Nehemiah 1:1-2 (KJV): *"The words of Nehemiah the son of Hachaliah. and it came to pass in the month chisleu, in the twentieth year, as I was in Shushan the palace, that Hanani, one of my brethren, came, he and certain men of Judah; and I asked them concerning the Jews that had escaped, which were left of the captivity, and concerning Jerusalem."*

The above is the story of how Nehemiah asked people about the situation of fellow Jews in Jerusalem during his time in captivity. From the response he obtained, he developed a vision to rebuild the walls of Jerusalem. His decision to pursue rebuilding the walls of Jerusalem did not come from any human persuasion or pressure; rather, it came within him. Nehemiah chose by himself to rebuild the walls of Jerusalem. He has a personal conviction for his vision.

It is important that you identify the source of your vision. It is possible to develop a vision based on envy or pressure from people in your life. The problem is that when your vision faces serious challenges, you may find it easy to drop it because it never came from within you; thereby, there is no inner conviction that could help you to fight the resistance. Nehemiah was able to resist every frustration that his vision faced because he had an inner conviction that the vision was the right thing to pursue. He was not running the race of another man or a race given to him from another place. It came from within him, and thereby, there was an inner strength through conviction to pursue the vision irrespective of external opposition.

If you want your vision to succeed, let it originate from the inside of you—where the Holy Spirit dwells. Be your real self; don't run the race of another man. Do not try to be like somebody else; be authentic.

I pray that the grace of God will make you the person God created you to be in Jesus' name.

4. Believer's mind.

This is a kind of a mind that believes in God. It is filled with faith and trust in God.

To believe means to have confidence in the reliability of somebody or something without absolute proof.

Genesis 15:6 (KJV): *"And he believed in the lord; and he counted it to him for righteousness."*

Abraham walked with God with confidence that God is reliable even when he had no proof of it.

Genesis 12:1 (KJV): *"Now the Lord had said unto Abram, get thee out of thy country, and from thy kindred, and from thy father's house, unto a land that I will shew thee."*

The above Bible verse showed the first time Abraham interacted with God; yet, he believed God's instruction.

It should be noted that Abraham did not come from the family of those who believed in God, but despite the lack of any previous evidence of who God was, he still believed God. He agreed with God to move from the familiar to the unfamiliar with the belief and obedience to a God he did not know. This is remarkable.

Genesis 13:14-15 (KJV): *"And the Lord said unto Abram, after that lot was separated from him, lift up now thine eyes, and look from the place where thou art northward, and southward, and eastward, and* *westward: for all the land which thou seest, to thee will I give it, and to thy seed for ever."*

After Lot has taken the seemingly good land, God told Abraham he would give him the seemingly barren land. Despite the ugly appearance of the land, Abraham still trusted what God said. He has confidence in God.

Similarly,

Genesis 22:1-2 (KJV): *"And it came to pass after these things, that God did tempt Abraham, and said unto him, Abraham: and he said, behold, here I am. and he said, take now thy son, thine only son Isaac, whom thou lovest, and get thee into the land of Moriah; and offer him there for a burnt offering upon one of the mountains which I will tell thee of."*

God told Abraham to sacrifice his only son to him; yet, Abraham still believed and obeyed God. Even though this instruction of God seemed to negate the initial promise God gave him that this very son, Isaac, will become a great nation, despite that, Abraham believed God in this seemingly contradictory situation.

The examples above made it clear that it is Abraham's nature to trust God's word.

Many Christians fail in vision because they could not believe God as they come across different situations. When God asks them to start their project without money, that He would supply them money when time matures, they will not start because they did not believe what God told them.

Furthermore, when God gives them further guidance that will help their vision, they ignore it because they did not trust what they heard from God. Many people also find it difficult to trust the messengers of God which He sends to help them in their vision.

2 Chronicles 20:20 (KJV): *"And they rose early in the morning, and went forth into the wilderness of Tekoa: and as they went forth, Jehoshaphat stood and said, hear me, o Judah, and ye inhabitants of Jerusalem; believe in the lord your god, so shall ye be established; believe his prophets, so shall ye prosper."*

The above verse reveals that there are two persons you must always believe in your life: God and His prophets.

To be established means to bring into existence, and the word *prosper* means to be successful or flourish. When you believe God, your plan will be brought into existence, but when you believe His prophets, your existing plan begins to flourish.

Many people bring their vision only into existence due to their belief that it was God that instructed them to do it, but unfortunately, their vision is not prospering and successful because they miss continual guidance through God's prophets. The believers that trust God and His servants will not only enjoy God's touch to start a vision, but they will enjoy continual guidance through the servants of God.

Therefore, it is important that you develop believers' mind because it will help you never to miss the right way. When it becomes your attitude to believe God and the prophets He sends to you, you will see your vision not only being established but prospering.

I pray that the grace for you never to miss God's guidance shall locate you today in Jesus' name.

5. Workable mind.

A workable mind is a mind that can be taught how to function under certain situations. It is not every mind God can work on because He will never violate your free will.

Acts 13:22 (KJV): *"And when he had removed him, he raised up unto them David to be their king; to whom also he gave testimony, and said, I have found David the son of Jesse, a man after mine own heart, which shall fulfil all my will."*

The above Bible verse reveals that God chose David because He saw that his heart is workable to Him. That is, if God shows him favour, he will also go and show favour to others. If God helps him, he will also help other people.

The workable mind is a mind that can be taught by example how to function under certain situations. God's expectation concerning you is that if He can be so good to you, you must also be good to Him and people. If God can be so generous to you, you must also be generous to Him and people.

2 Samuel 7:18 (KJV): *"Then went king David in, and sat before the Lord, and he said, who am I, o Lord God? And what is my house, that thou hast brought me hitherto?"*

King David considered how God has been so good to him and his household. He was overwhelmed by the kindness God has shown to him and his family. His heart was moved for him to enjoy such unconditional love.

2 Samuel 9:3 (KJV): *"And the king said, is there not yet any of the house of Saul, that I may shew the kindness of god unto him? And Ziba said unto the king, Jonathan hath yet a son, which is lame on his feet."*

In the above example, King David chose to show kindness to people, including those from his enemy's house. This act of kindness from David could be traced to the kind of kindness he received from God. It worked upon his heart/mind, influencing him to do the same to fellow human beings. Divine love taught him to show love to others. Can your mind be worked on by God to achieve a vision? Do you have a teachable heart? If you do not have a teachable heart, you will keep making the same error despite receiving guidance. People that do not have a workable mind will not learn from past mistakes. They will keep making the same mistake because their minds never accept correction and make an amendment. Do not forget or reject lessons life is teaching you. You will need a workable mind to succeed in your vision. You will need a mind that can change for the better. Do not be rigid but flexible in your thinking. Permit entrance of fresh ideas that you did not know before. Allow your mind to be convinced of a new way of doing things. Embrace new ideas and methods. Do not limit yourself to what you know only. There is more knowledge out there that can help your vision. Welcome new ideas, and do not be negative when you come across the knowledge you do not know before. Do not say your method is the only method available. If your method fails, seek another.

May your mind be workable and receptive to new ideas in Jesus' name.

6. Possibility mind.

This is a kind of mind that is so courageous that it sees the possibility of success despite all the hindrances. It believes that situations will work out well despite prevailing negative circumstances.

Numbers 14:6-9 (KJV): *"And Joshua the son of nun, and Caleb the son of Jephunneh, which were of them that searched the land, rent their clothes: and they spake unto all the company of the children of Israel, saying, the land, which we passed through to search it, is an exceeding good land. if the lord delight in us, then he will bring us into this land, and give it us; a land which floweth with milk and honey. only rebel not ye against the lord, neither fear ye the people of the land; for they are bread for us: their defence is departed from them, and the lord is with us: fear them not.*

In the above Bible story, truly, the Amalekites were giants, but Joshua and Caleb saw the possibility of defeating them. In Joshua 3, when Israel came across the overflowing river Jordan, Joshua was not moved by it, but rather, he saw the possibility of Israel crossing over the river.

Similarly, in Joshua 6, when Israel came across the wall of Jericho, Joshua was not moved by the walls because he saw the possibility of Israel bringing the walls down. In many situations, when Joshua faced battles, he faced them with the intention of attaining victory.

What made Joshua not to be afraid of danger?

Joshua 10:25 (KJV): *"And Joshua said unto them, fear not, nor be dismayed, be strong and of good courage: for thus shall the Lord do to all your enemies against whom ye fight."*

The above reveals that Joshua did not only have courage, but he also gave out courage to people. He was so courageous that he influenced other people around him to develop courage.

What is Courage?

Courage is the ability to do something irrespective of the danger. For example,

- → courageous people always see the possibility of the next move despite the lack of ideas. They believe that the next step is possible.
- → courageous people always see the possibility of overcoming a mountain despite the bigness of the mountain.
- → courageous people always see the possibility of moving forward despite all the roadblocks.
- → courageous people will see the possibility of defeating the strong opponent even though the opponent is stronger than them.

- → courageous people always see the possibility of crossing over to the other side of the road despite the big gulf that separates them from the other side. They believed that they would overcome the big gulf.
- → courageous people still see the possibility of good performance despite being under negative situations. They will always say: I will do well even when they face all negativities.
- → courageous people are difficult to be demotivated or made afraid.

Courage always sees possibility, and it always has a solution to every problem.

Matthew 19:26 (KJV): *"But Jesus beheld them, and said unto them, with men this is impossible; but with God all things are possible."*

Jesus said that despite whatever may come your way, everything is still possible for you. That is courage.

If you do not want your vision to collapse in the face of hindrances, develop courage. Face every difficult situation with a possibility mentality. Assure yourself that you are too strong to be stopped by fear or opposition. When you operate with a possibility mentality, then you will always have possibility. There will always be a solution to every problem. Possibility mentality opens your mind up for fresh ideas that bring solutions, while impossibility mentality closes your mind against the entrance of fresh ideas or solutions.

I pray that God will give you a mind of possibility in Jesus' name.

7. Peaceful mind.

This is a mind that operates in divine peace in all situations. There is power in calmness of the mind. A peaceful mind does not surrender to agitation, but it keeps its composure in the face of threat.

John 16:33 (KJV): *"These things I have spoken unto you, that in me ye might have peace. In the world ye shall have tribulation: but be of good cheer; I have overcome the world."*

In this Bible verse, Jesus was preparing the mind of the disciples for tribulation that will soon break out against them as they pursue the assignment God gave them. Few years after Jesus made this statement, persecution broke out against the disciples. Fortunately, all the persecution failed to stop the disciples from their assignment.

What kept disciples going during the time of persecution?

John 14:27 (KJV): *"Peace I leave with you, my peace I give unto you: not as the world giveth, give I unto you. Let not your heart be troubled, neither let it be afraid."*

The secret of disciples' triumph over persecution was divine peace. Jesus gave them divine peace to sustain them during tribulation. Divine peace is not of this world but heaven. You can only get divine peace when you relate with God.

Many people get confused and lose calmness whenever their vision comes under attack. This is because their mind lacks divine peace. A mind that lacks divine peace will easily get confused when faced challenges. If you want all your vision to always succeed, pray for divine peace. It calms the mind and head. For you to still be able to behave and function well when you face the adversary, you will need divine peace.

May God bless your heart with His peace in Jesus' name.

Prayer

- Father, the grace to complete all the good work you have made me start, release on me today in Jesus' name.
- Father, the power, energy, and courage to overcome every difficulty on my way, release on me today in Jesus' name.
- Father, let my mind be sound in all that I do in Jesus' name.
- Father, make all my vision speak and cause all my plans to be established in Jesus' name.
- Father, give me an enlightened mind, wise mind, authentic mind, believers' mind, workable mind, possibility mind, and peaceful mind in Jesus' name.

Chapter Five

Adjustments for the vision

Matthew 9:16-17 (KJV): *"No man putteth a piece of new cloth unto an old garment, for that which is put in to fill it up taketh from the garment, and the rent is made worse. Neither do men put new wine into old bottles: else the bottles break, and the wine runneth out, and the bottles perish: but they put new wine into new bottles, and both are preserved."*

These verses teach that it will be incompatible to mix the old with the new. This is because if we mix them, there will be a noticeable divergence between the old and the new. They will not mix well together. This implies that if your vision will be achieved, you will need to first identify the new and the old and separate them from each other for effectiveness' sake. When you start pursuing your vision, you will be exposed to new experiences and encounters. These encounters will compel you to adjust certain areas of your life to accommodate the challenges and requirements of your new endeavour. Unless you adjust, it will be difficult for you to properly fit into your new vision in terms of fulfilling its demands. It is, therefore, important that you identify the areas of your life that you will need to improve or adjust to be able to attain the level required for you to succeed in your visions.

In this chapter, we shall examine some areas of your life you will need to adjust so that your vision will not suffer due to the incompatibility of different factors involved in pursuing your vision. There are things you will need to drop or improve on or exchange for better performance.

Examples of such factors that may require your adjustment or exchange or improvement are:

Thinking Pattern

You will act according to the way you think. If your thinking process gets corrupted, your reaction to situations will also get corrupted. If you suffer from a negative thinking pattern, you will need to adjust your thinking pattern. You will need to mature your thinking pattern by dealing with the way you think. A negative thinking pattern will hinder your ability to come up with good and sound ideas necessary for your vision to advance. Similarly, irrational thinking pattern will seriously mar the future of your vision. There are books that can help you to deal with your thinking pattern.

Attitude

Attitude is a manner of thinking, feeling, or behaving that reflects a state of mind or disposition. It is a behavioural pattern that originates from the way you think. It develops from your repeated character or behaviour. Attitude is what you do over and over, consciously, or unconsciously.

Attitude will affect the result of whatever you want to pursue in life. There is always an attitude condition to satisfy for every achievement in life. There is an attitude you will need to show to achieve certain things in life. Therefore, you may need to adjust your attitude to avoid spoiling things affecting your vision. Your attitude will affect how you handle or react to the following:

a) Failure:

You will need a good attitude when your visions seem to fail, and every effort you make is not working. A good attitude will help you to turn failure into an opportunity for better performance.

b) Word of instruction:

You will need a good attitude to handle with maturity every word of instruction from people involved in your vision. When those who are more knowledgeable than you give you a word of instruction to help your vision, a good attitude will help you receive it with maturity.

c) Belief system:

You will need a good attitude to keep the faith that things will work out well for you despite series of complications. A wrong attitude will not let you demonstrate faith, especially when your hope seems to fade away. How is your belief system? Perhaps it may need serious adjustment to boost your faith.

d) Keep the fight:

You will need a good attitude to keep fighting opposition and hindrance until you defeat them. The way you react to frustration and challenges will determine whether you will escalate the matter or not. With a good attitude and calmness of the spirit, you can keep attacking enemies of your vision until you defeat them all. You will wisely put the situation under your control without escalating it.

e) Waiting:

Sometimes, you will need to practise waiting to get your plan through. Such waiting could be waiting for helpers or situations to mature naturally without interfering or for the right time to act. Good attitude will enable you to exhibit the patience necessary for your change to appear.

f) Focus:

When you maintain focus on your vision and resist distraction for a long time, your attitude will be tested. If you are someone who can't focus attention on a thing, then you will need to work on yourself. Your ability to concentrate on your mission is determined by your attitude.

g) Keep the praise:

In many situations, you will need to praise God or those helping your vision. But if you are a complainer that always murmurs, it will be difficult for you to praise because you are difficult to please. Ungratefulness is a negative attitude people exhibit towards those they are supposed to appreciate. Your lack of praise may turn helpers of destiny into haters of destiny. You will need to adjust your attitude if you are naturally an ungrateful person.

h) Keep the good expectations:

As you are pursuing your vision, you will need to keep expecting good things to happen to your vision so that your fire of hope will keep burning. You will need to keep expecting that ugly situations will soon turn out well. You should also expect helpers to come your way. If you keep good expectation, you will keep positive thinking. Your attitude will determine how long you can expect good things. When people stop expecting good things, they become negative. You may need to change your attitude so that you can keep expecting good things as regards your vision. When you expect good things and those good things manifest, you will not miss them. I advise you that you keep thinking good and keep expecting good.

Management:

Your act of handling, controlling, and supervising certain resources in your custody will have direct or indirect consequences on your vision. Lack of proper management skill will hinder how effective you can use or manipulate certain resources. For example, it will reduce the period your vision will take before it is fully matured if you can manage time effectively. Waste of time will prolong and cause an undue delay in the progress of your vision. It is important that you honestly evaluate your time management skill.

Furthermore, your ability to manage useful resources such as finance will determine the outcome of your vision. If you waste your little and scarce finances, it will reduce the amount of money available for you to spend on your visions. Many plans suffer because of wasteful spending. If you are too prodigal in handling money, you will need to educate yourself about managing financial resources; otherwise, your vision may die due to financial suffocation.

Crisis management is crucial if you can control ugly situations that may suffice as you pursue your vision. Sometimes, things do not go as expected. Challenges may occur. Oppositions may come from certain people that are envious of your vision. People that disagree with you may decide to create confusion and problems to frustrate your vision. Your ability to control crisis without permitting crisis to control you will be an asset to you. One of the major cautions when dealing with a crisis is not to escalate it. Never pour fuel inside a burning fire. You need to learn how to handle those that disagree with your vision without giving them more justification to hinder you. Be wise.

Routine:

What you do regularly will affect how much time and focus you will give to your vision. You may need to adjust your routine so that you can give better attention to your vision. Your routine could include what you do daily, weekly, monthly, and yearly. If your schedule is too tight such that you will not be able to apportion better time for your vision, it will prolong the time your vision will take to manifest. In other for you to adjust your routine, you will need to be honest to yourself in terms of time frame you expect your vision to get completed. For you to meet your time deadline, you must be ready to pay the sacrifice of making your vision an important part of your routine. Some visions require regular attention daily, and unless you give much time to it, things will be delayed beyond normal. You will need to adjust your daily schedule of events and re-allocate better time to your vision so that you will be able to accomplish it in record time.

Priority:

This is established by order of importance and urgency. If your vision will be achieved at the appropriate time, you will need to get your priority right. Some things are important but not urgent. Things that are important but not urgent need to be placed below the frontline on your schedule. Similarly, some things are major while others are minor. When you get your priority right, you will be able to identify major from minor and allocate time to them appropriately. Right priority enables you to first deal with major and then come back to minor later. When achieving a vision becomes your priority, you will be ready to set aside everything and focus totally on your vision. This is what enables great achievers to record success at the right time. They set aside every other thing and gave their entire attention to their vision. This promoted concentration and commitment which yielded encouraging success in a shorter time. Getting your priority right will save a lot of time. Therefore, when you develop a vision, you will need to adjust the list of your priority. Reset your priorities to promote your new visions.

Choice making:

You will need to adjust your choices to accommodate your new visions. Choice making becomes important when you face many options, and you must select among them. Will you select choices that will promote your vision or not? For example, if you develop a vision for your children that will require your regular attention and then you are faced with the option of two jobs. One will reduce your contact with your children and the other will permit regular contact though the salary of one seems greater than the other, which option will you choose? If making more money is of priority to you than helping your children become the kind of persons you want them to be, you are likely to choose jobs that will bring you more money and rob you of regular contact with your children. There are some difficult choices you may have to make if you truly want to achieve your vision. For example, you may have to get ready to miss certain privileges to promote the attainment of your vision.

Furthermore, you may need to let go of a certain relationship that will harm your vision if you genuinely want your vision to come to maturity. This is because some people will hinder your vision because of envy and jealousy. You should be clever enough to identify factors that will hinder your vision and avoid them. In your choice making, you must be intentional. Right choices can't be based on chances but intentionality. You must intentionally choose certain things while you drop another. For example, to have more time for your vision, you may have to intentionally reduce the time you spend on leisure. Devote more time to your vision and avoid things that waste your precious limited time.

Maturity:

This is a product of full development. When you grow in the way you handle certain things, you are maturing, but when you're fully grown up such that you do not lack any virtue as regards the indices, then you are fully matured. It takes time to reach the level of full maturity in any life endeavour, but it must be the target. You may need to adjust your way of handling certain things to advance your maturity in that regard. For example, you may need to mature your emotions and how you react to situations. When vision seems to fail, some people become negative, and this messes up the plans. Unregulated emotional reaction to shock or strange occurrences may destroy your vision. Get yourself collected and stabilise your emotion so that you will be able to control situations instead of situations controlling you.

Furthermore, you may need to mature your ways of doing things by doing one thing at a time to avoid muddling things together. It is lack of maturity when you want to do many things at a time. This will create confusion and a lack of direction. It is advisable that you handle one thing at a time. That is why it is better for you to break your visions down into various components and

Adjustments for the vision

deal with each at a time. When the whole vision is broken down into various components, you can decide about the best method to adopt. Each component may require a different method.

Similarly, to achieve maturity in all areas of your life, you may need to adjust your focus ability. If your focus is defective, you will have many blind spots, which will make you always ignore important things. When you notice that you usually ignore important things, it implies that there is a need for you to sharpen your focal power.

Finally, you may need to adjust how you test your work. As you progress with your vision, you will need to constantly test your work to check its progress. In testing your work, you will need to be honest with yourself. If you always score the progress of your vision excellent, you may need to re-evaluate your method of testing so that you will not be operating under self-deception.

How is your skill set? Your vision will demand certain skills and abilities from you. You must improve yourself in terms of skills so that you will be in a better position to help your vision. Therefore, before you embark on your vision, find out the skill demand the vision will place on you, and if you discover that you lack part of them, choose to improve yourself. Acquire whatever skills and abilities you lack before you embark on your vision.

Also, sometimes, if your vision will require working with a team, you may need to adjust your team members. If some of the team members lack certain skills, you may need to deal with that before you start allocating responsibility to each member. Otherwise, you will promote professional error that may frustrate your vision.

Prayer

- Holy Spirit, adjust my thinking pattern to suit the purpose of God for my life in Jesus' name.
- Father, strengthen me for my vision and empower me to fulfil my destiny in Jesus' name.
- Father, give me a fighting spirit never to give up my vision in Jesus' name.
- Father, make me stronger than failure in Jesus' name.
- Father, give me the grace to become the person You designed me to be in Jesus' name.

Chapter Six

Knowledge for the vision

Hosea 4:6 (KJV): *"My people are destroyed for lack of knowledge: because thou hast rejected knowledge, I will also reject thee, that thou shalt be no priest to me: seeing thou hast forgotten the law of thy God, I will also forget thy children."*

The Bible verse above reveals that lack of relevant knowledge leads to destruction. Such destruction could be of vision, plan, dreams, resources, and lives. Lack of relevant knowledge makes you very vulnerable to error and any type of danger. Without necessary knowledge about your vision, you will soon run into serious complications. The future of any good plan depends on the depth of knowledge the builder has. It is, therefore, important that before you embark on your vision, you should seek relevant knowledge. Never start building when you don't even know what you are building. Ensure that you educate yourself thoroughly before you embark on your vision. Whatever plan you have, ensure that you acquire the necessary knowledge before starting to work on it. Do not underestimate the power of knowledge when it comes to success in vision.

In this chapter, we want to examine various sources that you can explore to gain the necessary knowledge that will help you in your vision.

Examples of such knowledge are:

A. The Revealed knowledge.

This is the knowledge you received from the Holy Spirit about what you are doing. As you pray about your vision, presenting it before God for direction, the Holy Spirit will speak into your heart certain revelation necessary for your vision.

Paul showed us examples of such revealed knowledge you must have to position yourself to be able to deal with any new challenge that may come in your ways. Such revealed knowledge includes:

→ Ultimate vision

This is the knowledge about your expected end—the final result you aspire to achieve. This kind of knowledge exposes to you the end from the beginning. It helps you gain insight into how your vision will look like when it is fully fulfilled.

It helps you to see where you are going before you start the journey of your vision.

Philippians 3:10 (KJV): *"That I may know him, and the power of his resurrection, and the fellowship of his sufferings, being made conformable unto his death."*

According to the above, Paul cast a vision of his expected end in terms of achievement—to know Jesus more and to experience the power of His resurrection. This was the end he had in mind as he was progressing in his ministry. Similarly, if you can prayerfully approach God about your vision, He will show you how the end will be as regards your vision. When you see from the eyes of the Spirit how the beauty of your fully matured vision will look like, it will motivate you to progress with determination. You will progress, looking forward to the time when your vision will be born. It is like a pregnant woman that has seen the scan of her baby. She will keep looking forward to the day she will bring the child forth into physical existence.

→ Price visions

This is the knowledge of prices you will have to pay for you to achieve your expected end.

When you knew ahead of time the price you must pay to achieve your plan, it will not be a shock to you when the time comes for you to pay the price.

Acts 9:16 (KJV): *"For I will shew him how great things he must suffer for my name's sake."*

Paul received the visions of the price he must pay to attain his ultimate vision—he has to be ready to face diverse kind of sufferings.

Your own price may include overlooking insult, coping with hunger and sleeplessness, trekking for a long distance to get to certain places, or denying yourself certain privileges. Therefore, before you embark on your vision, explore the price tags.

→ Work vision

This is the knowledge of the kind of work you must do to achieve your purpose. This will educate you ahead of time on how laziness can frustrate your journey.

Acts 23:11 (KJV): *"And the night following the Lord stood by him, and said, be of good cheer, Paul: for as thou hast testified of me in Jerusalem, so must thou bear witness also at Rome."*

Paul obtained visions about the kind of work he will need to perform as part of his mission, which was an integral part of fulfilling his ultimate vision.

You will need to know the kind of work your vision requires so that when the demand for works comes, you will not quit. From the onset, get knowledge about work requirements and the aspect that will demand energy from you. There are some aspects of the work another person can do for you, but there will be one you have to do personally. It will be an error for you to expect another person to do for you what you must do personally.

→ Vision of challenges

This is the knowledge about the likely challenges on the way, such as opposition and hindrances you may encounter.

When you knew ahead of time the nature of challenges on the way, you will not be caught unawares when they begin to manifest.

Acts 22:18 (KJV): *"And saw him saying unto me, make haste, and get thee quickly out of Jerusalem: for they will not receive thy testimony concerning me."*

Paul received visions of possible challenges. This will help him not to worry if he encounters any hindrances.

When you understand possible hindrances that you may encounter on the way when they start manifesting, you will turn them to motivation instead of discouragement.

→ Vision of Assurance

This is an assurance from the Holy Spirit of divine assistance for success.

When you knew that the Lord would fight for you in all challenges ahead of time, you will exhibit a positive attitude when challenges come.

Acts 18:9-10 (KJV): *"Then spake the Lord to Paul in the night by a vision, be not afraid, but speak, and hold not thy peace: for I am with thee, and no man shall set on thee to hurt thee: for I have much people in this city."*

Paul received from the Lord the visions of peace to assure him that his effort will not fail.

You need to learn how to wait for peace from the Holy Spirit before you start your journey. This is to assure you of divine assistance when challenges come. Do not start until there is peace inside of you. When you have peace before you, embark on your vision. It is an assurance that God will help you on the way because He is in support of your plan. Do not embark on a journey without first receiving peace in the heart from the Holy Spirit as an assurance of divine approval of your plan. God would not fight for you if He did not approve your plan.

Finally, Acts 26:19 reveals that Paul obeyed every vision and revelational knowledge he received from the Holy Spirit.

Acts 26:19 (KJV): *"Whereupon, o king Agrippa, I was not disobedient unto the heavenly vision."*

Similarly, you need to write down every revelation you received. Ensure that you do not despise such knowledge, for it will be a guide for you in the days ahead.

B. Written knowledge

This is the knowledge written inside books—book knowledge.

This is the knowledge you received through reading and the personal research you have done before and during your journey.

Such books include Bible and other non-religious books such as science, history, etc.

Daniel 9:2 (KJV): *"In the first year of his reign I Daniel understood by books the number of the years, whereof the word of the LORD came to Jeremiah the prophet, that he would accomplish seventy years in the desolations of Jerusalem."*

Through the reading of books, Daniel gained access to the hidden knowledge he required for his pursuit in Babylon.

Acts 7:22 (KJV): *"And Moses was learned in all the wisdom of the Egyptians, and was mighty in words and in deeds."*

Ahead of time, Moses had studied Egyptians' culture and traditions.

When he faced the Egyptians to liberate Israel, he knew the people he was dealing with ahead of time. All the opposition Moses faced from Pharaoh and all the wise men of Egypt did not meet Moses by surprise. He knew them and how to respond to their challenges.

Hebrews 12:1 (KJV): *"Wherefore seeing we also are compassed about with so great a cloud of witnesses, let us lay aside every weight, and the sin which doth so easily beset us, and let us run with patience the race that is set before us."*

Witnesses are people that had passed through the same route you are passing through or about to pass through. Through books, you will discover those who had done the same thing you are about to do and how they failed or succeeded. You will discover what they did wrongly and rightly. You will then learn from them so that you can have their success and escape their failure.

Similarly, you could also discover better information about your plan through books. This will help you to reflect and evaluate yourself whether you are fit for the plan or not. Through books, you can make an informed decision.

C. Observed Knowledge

This is the knowledge you will gather through observation, using your physical eyes. This includes real events that God will enable you to witness to teach you certain knowledge.

Numbers 13:17-20 (KJV): *"And Moses sent them to spy out the land of Canaan, and said unto them, Get you up this way southward, and go up into the mountain: And see the land, what it is; and the people that dwelleth therein, whether they be strong or weak, few or many; And what the land is that they dwell in, whether it be good or bad; and what cities they be that they dwell in, whether in tents, or in strong holds; And what the land is, whether it be fat or lean, whether there be wood therein, or not. And be ye of good courage and bring of the fruit of the land. Now the time was the time of the first ripe grapes."*

In the above Bible story, the Israelites were to spy on the land they were about to occupy. They were to enter the city and observe the situation; the information they will gather will then be used to make some vital decisions.

There are times God expects you to use your physical eyes to observe situations He is showing you so that you can gain more knowledge about your plan. When God enables you to witness some real-life events or hear some messages from people around you, it is to help you gain further knowledge that could help your vision. You will not need to ignore situations God has brought before you to see. From such exposure, you are to make a logical conclusion and wise decisions.

For example, as a lady, you are planning to marry a man that you have witnessed constantly maltreating his parents and disrespecting his relatives. This could be that God is showing you something to help you to make a wise decision. It could be that God is showing you that when you marry him, he will treat you as he has been treating his own relatives.

Never forget the knowledge you acquired through observation that could promote your vision.

D. Knowledge from created things such as nature, animals, trees, etc.

This is the knowledge you gained by studying created things.

Proverbs 30:25 (KJV): *"The ants are a people not strong, yet they prepare their meat in the summer."*

The above Bible verse says that a wise man with foresight is compared with an ant. Such a man will plan for the dry season during the rainy season.

He will plan for the days of lack during the time of his days of abundance. That is wisdom from studying an ant.

Psalm 1:3 (KJV): *"And he shall be like a tree planted by the rivers of water, that bringeth forth his fruit in his season; his leaf also shall not wither; and whatsoever he doeth shall prosper."*

From this verse, a righteous man is compared to a tree planted by the riverside. It implies that by studying a tree planted on the side of the waters, we can learn a lot about a righteous man.

Matthew 10:16 (KJV): *"Behold, I send you forth as sheep in the midst of wolves: be ye therefore wise as serpents, and harmless as doves."*

In this scripture, believers are compared with serpents and dove. It means that as a believer, there are times to act as a serpent, and there are times to act as a dove. If you act as a serpent when you're supposed to act as a dove, you will make the situation worse.

Going through the Bible, there are many comparisons made between certain people and created things.

From some of the above comparison, you can learn about the kind of nature you possess and how you are likely to act under certain situations.

Furthermore, when you study those created things and examine your nature, it gives you an idea of your inherent human and regenerated nature.

For example, if your nature is totally like a lamb, you are likely to give up a plan easily when your plan hit the rock or faces strong opposition.

This is because a lamb loves peace and hates war; it runs away from trouble.

Imagine a person of mostly lamb nature who wants to choose a career that will involve constant exposure to terrible and hard people. It is a matter of time before he will soon give up. He will not be able to do the 'fire for fire' approach because of his gentle nature. Similarly, imagine a person of mostly lion-like nature who wants to get engaged in an endeavour requiring dealing with different kind of people, both strong and weak. Lions only get along well with fellow lions because you rarely see other animals befriend lions because of fear of being eaten as food.

Therefore, such a person will soon discover that many people that do not have lion-like nature like him will be running away from him. He will soon give up his endeavour due to frustration that some people don't like him. Nobody wants to associate with a lion except other lions.

This implies that before you embark on any vision, try to learn about your nature to find out how you will perform as you come across different circumstances.

E. Relational Knowledge

This is the knowledge you acquire through the relationship between you and fellow human beings.

What people say or the opinion they conceived about you could help you in your purpose.

Matthew 16:13-15 (KJV): *"When Jesus came into the coasts of Caesarea Philippi, he asked his disciples, saying, Whom do men say that I the Son of man am? And they said, Some say that thou art John the Baptist: some, Elias; and others, Jeremias, or one of the prophets. He saith unto them, But whom say ye that I am?"*

From the above verses, after a long period of dealing with people, Jesus asked His disciples how people perceived Him—who they consider Him to be.

Now that people have witnessed His performance and tasted His goodness, they must have developed a certain opinion about Him. Jesus was interested in what people and disciples thought of Him.

This is important because before He started His ministry or shortly after He started, some people saw Him as Jesus the son of Joseph or somebody from Nazareth, where nothing good can come from. But after witnessing series of miracles through Him, their opinion must have changed.

Note that people's opinion will affect their level of acceptance of you. Without acceptance, you can't save or deliver anybody from their captivity.

You need to understand how people's opinion about you could affect your vision. There are visions that will expose you to working or relating with people. Some visions will require that you form a team to work with. Therefore, the way people see you will influence their interaction with you. For example, when people start working against your plan to frustrate you, it is because of the way they see you. Similarly, when people start promoting your plan, it is because of the way they see you.

Many people give up a good plan, not because they were not good enough to achieve the plan, but because the people they were dealing with rose against them due to the way they saw them.

If you will succeed in your plan, you must be mindful of what people you are dealing with think or conceive in their hearts about you because it will affect their attitude towards you and your plan.

F. Knowledge through exposure to circumstances of life

This is the knowledge gained through situations that God has exposed you to, such as trial, failure, success, rejection, acceptance, fear, etc. There are many things you can learn from life experiences and exposures that will aid your vision.

For example, David confessed that he had become a better person through the trials he faced, according to:

Psalm 119:71 (KJV): *"It is good for me that I have been afflicted; that I might learn thy statutes."*

There are certainly some changes David must have observed in himself that made him make such a conclusion. This will help him in future decisions.

What have you learned from your past life trials?

Furthermore, through success and great achievement, Solomon has discovered the vanity of life, according to:

Ecclesiastes 1:13-14 (KJV): *"And I gave my heart to seek and search out by wisdom concerning all things that are done under heaven: this sore travail hath God given to the sons of man to be exercised therewith. I have seen all the works that are done under the sun; and, behold, all is vanity and vexation of spirit."*

This kind of knowledge will no doubt shape the way Solomon will pursue the future ambition. He is likely to be more thoughtful as he approached life situations.

Also, Israel was exposed to hunger to gather the knowledge that man can't live by bread alone but by the word of God, according to,

Deuteronomy 8:2-3 (KJV): *"And thou shalt remember all the way which the LORD thy God led thee these forty years in the wilderness, to humble thee, and to prove thee, to know what was in thine heart, whether thou wouldest keep his commandments, or no. And he humbled thee, and suffered thee to hunger, and fed thee with manna, which thou knewest not, neither did thy fathers know; that he might make thee know that man doth not live by bread only, but by every word that proceedeth out of the mouth of the LORD doth man live."*

This kind of exposure will educate Israelites to put their trust in God's word.

All the above biblical examples indicate that there are many things we can learn from different situations we are exposed to in life that could help us in our future decisions and pursuits. Some exposures will build your faith, while others will remind you of your vulnerabilities. If you have a record of failure in certain life pursuits and your new vision will require that you pass through the same exposure, you will need to revisit what happened in the past so that you do not commit the same error and experience the same blunders.

G. Impacted or transferred knowledge

This is the knowledge you gained from people more knowledgeable than you, such as a teacher/mentor.

Acts 22:3 (KJV): *"I am verily a man which am a Jew, born in Tarsus, a city in Cilicia, yet brought up in this city at the feet of Gamaliel, and taught according to the perfect manner of the law of the fathers, and was zealous toward God, as ye all are this day."*

The Bible verse above indicates that Paul had a teacher called Gamaliel who taught him about the law. This kind of impartation was secular, not spiritual. Paul later became a competent lawyer regarding the law of Moses, but this never made him a spiritual person with the fear of God.

Acts 9:17 (KJV): *"And Ananias went his way, and entered into the house; and putting his hands on him said, Brother Saul, the Lord, even Jesus, that appeared unto thee in the way as thou camest, hath sent me, that thou mightest receive thy sight, and be filled with the Holy Ghost."*

Here also, Paul was later mentored by Ananias about the way of the Lord. This kind of impartation was spiritually designed to make Paul a better person useful in God's hand.

We can then conclude from the above that Gamaliel belongs to the flesh who mentored Paul about secular knowledge. In contrast, Ananias belongs to the Spirit who mentored Paul about spiritual things.

For every plan to succeed, you will need to get engaged with someone that can teach you in the secular and another that will teach you in the spirit. You need one mentor to impact the secular knowledge related to your plan and a spiritual mentor to give you spiritual guidance along the journey.

H. Foundational Knowledge

This is the knowledge you gained through life preparation, such as where you were raised up.

Hebrews 11:23-27 (KJV): *"By faith Moses, when he was born, was hid three months of his parents, because they saw he was a proper child; and they were not afraid of the king's commandment. By faith Moses, when he was come to years, refused to be called the son of Pharaoh's daughter; Choosing rather to suffer affliction with the people of God, than to enjoy the pleasures of sin for a season; Esteeming the reproach of Christ greater riches than the treasures in Egypt: for he had respect unto the recompense of the reward. By faith he forsook Egypt, not fearing the wrath of the king: for he endured, as seeing him who is invisible."*

Moses was brought up in the palace of Pharaoh, the same place where his future assignment will start from. Moses' engagement was to give him a solid foundation and prepare him for his future assignment.

You need to understand that many plans fail because the person did what God has not prepared him or her for.

It is advisable that before you engage in any new plan, check your past to see if God has prepared you for it. Generally, before God will ask you to pursue anything, there will always be something He has done in your past to prepare you for the future.

Therefore, before you start a journey, try to look back and explore how God has been dealing with you in the past. There must be something in your past that prepared you for the future.

Many give up a plan because they are doing what God has never prepared them for.

Prayer

- Father, release on me today the spirit of wisdom and revelation in Jesus' name.
- Father, anoint me with the spirit of excellence in Jesus' name.
- Holy Spirit, help me to always retain, remember, and apply appropriately every knowledge I receive from the word of God in Jesus' name.
- Father, let your light dwell within me in all my days in Jesus' name.
- Father, arise and overthrow any demonic power that wants to steal the good seeds you planted in me in Jesus' name.

Chapter Seven

The visionary and the change

In previous chapters, we have defined a visionary as a person that sees into the future. Vision is about who you see yourself becoming in future.

The new person you see yourself becoming will require new things happening in your life or around you to enable you to become that new person.

Certain changes must take place in and around you for you to become a new person as regards your vision for your life.

Let us use the case of Joseph as it is revealed from Genesis Chapter 37 of the Bible.

In Genesis 37, Joseph had a dream in which he saw himself becoming a new person. He saw himself in an exalted position where his brothers bowed before him.

To become this new person, Joseph experienced seven major changes in his life.

Similarly, if you will become the new person you see yourself becoming, you will need to aspire to attain these changes as they happened in Joseph's life.

Those seven changes are:

1. Joseph lost the familiar

To be the person he saw himself to be in a dream, Joseph must lose certain things he was familiar with, which are:

→ Positional glory

Positional glory is the glory you received, not because of what you did but because of a certain position you occupy.

Genesis 37:23 (KJV): *"And it came to pass, when Joseph was come unto his brethren, that they stript Joseph out of his coat, his coat of many colours that was on him."*

Here, it revealed that Joseph was the last born of Jacob and his father made for him a robe of many colours. This means Joseph was special among his brothers.

It also revealed that when Joseph's brothers wanted to sell him, they took away his robe of many colours, signifying that he has lost his positional glory in the family.

→ Foundational bond

This is the bond existing between you and certain people because of your birthplace.

In Genesis 37:28, Joseph was sold to slavery by his brothers. This robbed him of his bond with his relatives, especially his father, who loved him so much.

The good news is that in Genesis 45 when Joseph became fulfilled, he regained back all he has lost in the past in a better form. All his relatives came to join him in Egypt, and he regained the bond he has lost. Also, he regained his lost glory and gained another glory of being the prime minister of a foreign country.

In fact, in Egypt, he had two forms of glory when he achieved his vision: he had positional glory (which he received by virtue of his position in the family) and acquired glory (the glory he received due to what he did in Egypt).

The story of Joseph teaches us that if we are going to become the person we wanted to be, we should be ready to lose our positional glory. You may have certain glory and honour based on your position in the family, among brethren, friends, place of employment, etc., but if you want to become a new person far better than your present position, you must be ready to temporarily let go of your present position. Otherwise, the pride of it may hinder you from being humble enough to become the new person which you desired.

The lesson here is that whatever you lose to become the person you wanted to be, you shall regain it in a bigger form. Therefore, if you really want to be the person you have never been before, you must get ready to lose certain things you are familiar with, at least, temporarily.

Philippians 2:5-9 (KJV): *"Let this mind be in you, which was also in Christ Jesus: who, being in the form of God, thought it not robbery to be equal with God: but made himself of no reputation, and took upon him the form of a servant, and was made in the likeness of men: and being found in fashion as a man, he humbled himself, and became obedient unto death, even the death of the cross. Wherefore God also hath highly exalted him and given him a name which is above every name."*

Jesus had glory in heaven, but He relinquished it to fulfil His vision of becoming the Saviour of the world, but when He achieved His vision, He regained the glory back but in a bigger form. Jesus was placed in an exalted position—the position greater than the one He occupied before He came to save the world. So, Jesus regained His positional glory—the one He had by virtue of being the only begotten Son, and He also gained acquired glory, the glory He gained by what He did in dying for humanity.

Therefore, in order for you to fulfil your vision, you may need to get ready to lose certain things you are familiar with, such as certain privileges, opportunities, position, possession, practice you enjoy, the treatment you enjoy, certain association, certain comfort, certain gains, etc. When your vision is fulfilled, you will regain back all you might have lost in a greater magnitude. All these are the prices of destiny every visionary pays.

2. Change of masters

For Joseph to become the person he saw in his dream, he found himself changing masters.

For example, in Genesis 39:1-3, Mr Potiphar became the master of Joseph, and shortly after that, the keeper of the prison became the master of Joseph in Genesis 39:20-23. Later in Genesis 41:39-44, King Pharaoh became the master of Joseph.

There was a change of master as Joseph was moving closer to the fulfilment of his dream.

A master is the person who has authority over another person. Your master is the person who has become the person you are aspiring to be in future.

For example, if you want to become an engineer, you will need a master who is already an engineer. Your master is a tutor, a coach, instructor, a leader, a guide, etc. Your master shows you the way up and helps you to become the person you aspire to be. You need to be aware that many people fail in destiny because they have no one to lead and show them the way to go. Whatever you want to achieve in life, somebody has already achieved it. Learn from the person.

I would like to state that you must know when to change master. For example, you will need to be changing masters as you desire to move higher. When you reach a position whereby the knowledge of your present master is limited, you will need a new master of higher knowledge.

For example, the person helping you in mathematics when you were preparing for your general certificate examination may not be qualified to keep helping you when you are now in the university—you need a more qualified master. Many people are not fulfilled today because they have no master or don't know when to change the master.

3. Change of association

To be fully grounded in his destiny, Joseph found himself changing association.

Genesis 39:22 (KJV): *"And the keeper of the prison committed to Joseph's hand all the prisoners that were in the prison; and whatsoever they did there, he was the doer of it."*

When Joseph was in prison, his associates were fellow prisoners, but in Genesis 41:45, when he was promoted as prime minister, he was given a wife—the daughter of a priest—not a prisoner. Joseph will now relate with credible and important people in the land—people already at the top. You can see that as Joseph was moving up the ladder of destiny, his associates kept changing to meet his new status in destiny.

Many people are not fulfilled in life because they still move with people they used to move with when they were little.

You need to understand that as God is moving you higher, you will need to change association. You will need to associate with people at your level or above your level.

When Paul met God in Acts 9, his association changed immediately.

Proverbs 27:17 (KJV): *"Iron sharpeneth iron; so a man sharpeneth the countenance of his friend."*

That is, good people help each other to become better. People you associate with can help you to become better in life. Therefore, separate from those that are not able to make you better in life. Many good people struggle in life because people they associate with are pulling them down both emotionally, mentally, and spiritually.

4. Change of assignments

To become the person he was destined to be, Joseph found himself facing different assignments.

In Genesis 39:5, Joseph took care of Mr Potiphar's household and business—both agricultural and non-agricultural. Also, in Genesis 39:22, Joseph started taking care of prisoners, and he later started taking care of the entire nation of Egypt from Genesis 41.

As he moved up the ladder of his dream, his assignment kept changing, getting bigger and bigger.

It should be noted that the purpose of different assignments for Joseph was to mature him and help him to acquire a good attitude and caring nature—which he would need if he were to become the person he saw in his dream.

It is written in Acts 15:18 that known unto God are all His

works from the beginning of the world. That is, God has a pre-knowledge about everything He has created. You are part of God's works He created. God knew when He was creating you, every desire, vision, and dream you will imagine and pursue all your days. Therefore, what God started doing in your life before you even conceived any vision was to expose you gradually to different situations that will help you to develop necessary skills for your vision and dream that you will develop in the future.

That is why it is crucial for you to look back into your past days, the kind of exposure God has given you before you start pursuing your vision and dream. God always prepares us ahead of time before we develop any vision or dream. Such preparation comes through personal and divine encounters.

5. Change of problems

Joseph moved from problem to problem before he became the person he saw in his dream.

In Genesis 37:4, when his brethren saw that their father loved him more than all his brethren, they hated him and could not speak peaceably unto him. He was hated by his own blood, and that problem of hatred developed until they sold him into slavery.

Furthermore, in Genesis 37, Joseph faced temptation when Mrs Potiphar asked him to sleep with her. Unfortunately, this problem developed until he was thrown into prison. Though Joseph did not yield to this temptation, he faced the negative consequences of his obedience to God.

In Genesis 40:15, Joseph voiced out his unfair treatment to the king's butler he met in prison. He explained to him the injustice he has suffered and that he had done nothing wrong to be thrown into prison.

The question is: why did God allow him to face a different kind of problems?

→ To teach him how to trust God in all situations—both negative and positive. In all his trials, Joseph never defended himself, for he has surrendered all to the Lord.

→ To help him to discover his moral weaknesses and strengths. Joseph must have learned by experience how to control his tongue because it was the lack of control of his tongue that made his brethren sell him into prison. If he kept quiet about his dream, they would not have hated him more.

→ To mature him. Genuinely matured people are humble. Joseph grew in maturity as he handled very well every stage of his trial. He did not fall into any of the traps devil arranged for him.

It was a divine plan that Joseph would face trials to make him a better person that would become the person he saw himself to be in his dream.

As it happened to Joseph, so it will happen to all God's children that pursue divine agenda for their lives.

Deuteronomy 8:2-3 (KJV): *"And thou shalt remember all the way which the LORD thy God led thee these forty years in the wilderness, to humble thee, and to prove thee, to know what was in thine heart, whether thou wouldest keep his commandments, or no. And he humbled thee, and suffered thee to hunger, and fed thee with manna, which thou knewest not, neither did thy fathers know; that he might make thee know that man doth not live by bread only, but by every word that proceedeth out of the mouth of the LORD doth man live."*

In the above verses, God led Israel through the wilderness. The wilderness is a place of series of problems and temptation. As they came out of one problem and temptation, they faced another until they became the people God wanted them to be.

When God gives you a vision, He also gives you problems, and unless you overcome those problems, the vision will not be fulfilled.

In Luke 4:1-2, our Lord Jesus Christ was not spared from this preparation through problems. He was led into the wilderness to be tempted by the devil, and after His triumph, He entered fully into His ministry. To be tempted by the devil means to face series of problems in isolation. Jesus was alone in the wilderness, facing series of attacks from the devil as part of His preparation for His destiny.

The temptation Jesus faced was divine. God organised it.

The success Jesus recorded from this encounter positioned Him to keep defeating the devil as he attempts to trouble Jesus in His ministry.

God exposes us to certain difficulty because He wants to make us better people so that when we occupy our position of glory, we will be too strong for the enemy to uproot.

Therefore, do not walk away from your vision because series of problems are coming your way. God has permitted those problems to make you a better person who will be able to fulfil His vision.

6. Change of name

Another change Joseph encountered was a change of name.

Genesis 41:45 (KJV): *"And Pharaoh called Joseph's name Zaphnath-paaneah; and he gave him to wife Asenath the daughter of Poti-pherah priest of On. And Joseph went out over all the land of Egypt."*

From the above verse, the name of Joseph was changed to Zaphnathpaaneah.

The meaning of Zaphnathpaanea in Hebrew is a *revealer of secrets*, while in Egypt, it is the *preserver of the age*.

Joseph's assignment in Egypt was to preserve Egyptians so that they will not perish during the seven years of famine, but it was his gift of interpreting the dream that opened that door for him. Joseph may have many other skills, but his skill of interpreting dreams was outstanding.

What is a name?

A name is used to identify somebody. For you to fulfil your vision, you will need to be identified with certain skills that link you to your visions.

For example, if you want to be an engineer, you will need to be identified with mathematical skills. Though you may have many other skills, your mathematical skill must be dominant.

Similarly, if you want to be a lawyer, you will need to be identified with communication skill. You may have many other skills, but communication skill must be dominant.

If your dominant skill can't be connected to your vision, you will struggle a lot.

There must be a connection between what you can do best and the major skill your vision/dream needed.

In Daniel 1:3-4, the king stated the major skill set required to select certain children of Israel. They may have many other skills, but they must be outstanding in knowledge and wisdom to apply that knowledge.

Therefore, before you embark on any vision/dream, check your best attributes so that you will not struggle.

7. Change of dress

Joseph experienced change of dress on his way to becoming the person he saw in his dream.

The visionary and the change

Genesis 41:14 (KJV): *"Then Pharaoh sent and called Joseph, and they brought him hastily out of the dungeon: and he shaved himself, and changed his raiment, and came in unto Pharaoh."*

According to the above, when Joseph was to appear before Pharaoh, he needed to change his prison dress.

In Genesis 41:42, when Joseph was to be put on a horse to be introduced to the nation of Egypt, they changed his dressing again—to fit into his office as a prime minister.

What is a dress?

A dress represents the way you appear before people or the way you introduce yourself to people. This includes your countenance, body language, mood, humility, smile, jokes, handshake, greetings, neatness, etc.

As you pursue your vision, you must understand that God will bring you before people that can promote your vision—they are called destiny helpers. The way you introduce yourself to such people can affect the quality of help you will receive.

A brother was going for an interview, and he decided to branch at his pastor's office to pray for him, but when the pastor saw him, he told him that they would not give him the job irrespective of the amount of prayer. The man was disappointed. The pastor told him that the reason is that his hair was untidy, his mouth was smelling, and the belt he used was not properly holding the trousers. His appearance disqualified him.

Even if you have all the qualifications, but your appearance betrays you, people that will assess you will develop a negative mindset based on your appearance. This negative mindset will affect any other judgements they will give about you. Your dressing matters if you are to fulfil your vision.

Below are the examples of clothes you must remove when you are appearing before destiny helpers.

- Cloth of affliction

In Mark 10:50, when Bartimaeus was to appear before Jesus for healing, he first removed his cloth of affliction.

When you are to appear before a destiny helper, don't bother him with all your problems and wounds; otherwise, you will make yourself unattractive and boring.

- Cloth of mourning

It is written in Isaiah 61:3 that God has given the garment of praise to those that mourn in Zion.

Those that mourn are those who are sorrowful due to their losses.

Do not approach helpers of your destiny with the appearance of a loser, full of angry look. Rather, put on a royal dressing as Esther did in Esther 5:1 when she was about to appear before the king for urgent help. This dressing made her irresistible to the king as the king could not overlook her radiant, lively, and attractive look.

Furthermore, **Ecclesiastes 9:8 (KJV)** states that: *"Let thy garments be always white; and let thy head lack no ointment."*

A white garment means to be spotless, while ointment means oil that smells nice.

This implies that you must appear before your helpers with a spotless dressing, including a nice and attractive smell. Let your helpers read who you are through your appearance.

Prayer

- Father, from now on, whenever helpers of my destiny set their eyes on me, let me be attractive to them in Jesus' name.
- Father, you are the God of change; whoever and whatever need to change for my vision and dream to be established, do it today in Jesus' name.
- Father, by your Spirit, work inside of me to be the person that I need to be for me to be fulfilled in Jesus' name.
- Father, the grace to persevere under every situation, let it locate me today in Jesus' name.
- Father, help me to separate from every wrong association capable of frustrating my vision in Jesus' name.

CHAPTER EIGHT

The pressures of a visionary

A visionary is a person that sees into the future and develops visions for his life. Vision is about who you are becoming in future. It is about what you see your job, career, ministry, marriage, business, and other aspects of your life become in the future.

Due to the interconnectivity that exists between human beings and their environment, nobody exists in isolation. There are other people or forces that will affect whatever you want to become in future. Some of these forces may exert a certain pressure on you to alter your vision. Therefore, it is important that you understand how these forces could affect your vision so that you will be able to handle them effectively without causing negative impacts on your vision.

Let us examine seven types of pressures that may affect your vision and how you can handle them.

1. The pressure of vision people developed for your life.

As you grow up in life, people that you contact may begin to develop plans indirectly or directly for your life. Some of these people may start to think about how your marriage should be, who your children should become, the kind of career you should choose, the kind of accommodation that will suit you, etc.

Sometimes, when you become aware of some of the plans people think about your life, it may put you under pressure when you begin to develop a plan for your own life, especially when your plan differs from what people think it should be.

For example, in Matthew 13:54-58, when those who knew Jesus from His youth saw Him doing miracles, they found it difficult to accept Him. They knew Him as a son of a carpenter, and in their expectation of Him, Jesus supposed to follow the path of His father to practise carpentry. To those people that knew Him, Jesus can only be the best in carpentry that He grew up seeing His father practising. Those people would have believed in Jesus if they saw Him doing carpentry because that would have fulfilled their expectation about Him.

Contrary to their expectation, they saw Him acting as a priest, and it became difficult for them to accept Him.

Due to fear of rejection, some people chose to dance to the expectation of those trying to design their lives.

Some years ago, my family dwelled in a two-bedroom flat in the town where we lived. After staying in this accommodation for many years, we decided to change to a three-bedroom house because of family expansion. When a friend of mine became aware of it, he was not happy that we have moved from smaller accommodation to a bigger one. We later discovered that this friend expected us to remain in the two-bedroom accommodation because it was cheaper than the bigger one we moved into. It was strange to my family that someone outside our home was designing the kind of accommodation that suits our situation.

As you relate with people, they silently develop expectations for your life. When they become aware that your vision is contrary to their expectation, some of them could become angry with you to the extent that they start rejecting you due to their disappointment regarding your vision. As a visionary, you should be courageous enough to move on with your visions. You hold no one any apology or explanation for choosing the kind of future you want for yourself. If such people try to put pressure on you to alter your visions to suit their expectation, you must resist unless you have inner conviction about their suggestion.

2. The pressure of the vision you develop to please people.

Sometimes, you may want to become something you know you are not comfortable with, but because you want to please certain people, you develop your vision to please them. You start pretending to be who you know you are not supposed to be. When you develop a vision to please the people in your life, this will build up pressure on you. You'll begin to fake things up in your life and become unreal in destiny. You will soon discover that this is not you, and you will start feeling the pressure of sustainability. It will become difficult for you to maintain the fake shape you develop to please those in your life.

A brother of mine chose to become a pastor because his wife told him to be one. This fellow became a pastor to please his wife. This person started faking attributes of a pastor, but those who have seen pastors before start wondering if this man was really a pastor. It was clear to those around him that this man has chosen a wrong vision because nothing in his personality proved that he was made to be the person he has become.

Furthermore, a friend of mine married a lady that his father chose for him. He did not want to disappoint his father, so he yielded to the pressure to marry a lady she was not in love with. After few years into the marriage, the relationship collapsed, and they divorced.

Never develop a vision to please people in your life. Otherwise, you will struggle to fit into it. When people pressure you to develop visions that you are not comfortable with, you should be courageous enough to refuse their suggestion. Never let life make you a surrogate in destiny. It is better for a man to refuse a vision to please others and be despised than for a man to choose a vision to please others and end it in disgrace. Also, avoid doing things that appear right, but yet, you are not happy doing it.

3. The pressure of vision you develop through assumptions.

There are people, including believers, that develop visions not because they have heard from God but because they observed the trend of events in their lives, made a conclusion out of it, and assumed that it is God's plan for their lives. Such people will develop a plan because they think that it is God's plan for their lives. They just observe the trend of events around their lives without any critical analysis of whether they possess attributes required to fulfil the visions. They run their lives with assumption   s.

A brother of mine chose to enter politics because people around him have been describing him as a person who possesses the attributes of a politician. He then concluded that God must have been speaking to him to go into politics. Unfortunately, after many failures in politics, he withdrew from it. He later discovered that he was not made for politics.

Never develop vision out of assumption but conviction.

In 1 Samuel 10:11-12, Saul prophesied among the prophets, but he was not a prophet. This one-off incident became a proverb in Israel, and people started saying: *Is Saul also among the prophets?* Nevertheless, Saul was not a prophet but a king.

Unfortunately, in 1 Sam. 13:8-14, when Samuel the priest was delayed to make sacrifices, Saul chose to perform his role. When Samuel came, he rebuked Saul vehemently and later Saul was removed as a king. Though Saul has been described as a prophet before, he was not ordained to be a prophet.

It is dangerous for you to develop a vision out of the assumption that comes only from an arrangement of events in your life.

As a believer, never conclude about God's position in your life by interpreting the trend of events only. Ensure you seek confirmation from God. The fact that God gives you certain exposure does not mean that God wants you to become somebody in that exposure.

A man discovered that a lady was always engaging him in conversation, and from that incident, he started thinking that the lady was interested in marrying him. This man later heard that the lady had married another man. He was very disappointed and angry.

As a visionary, you should avoid putting yourself under pressure through assumption. Stop observing signs but wait for God to speak clearly into your heart.

4. The pressure of vision you develop due to deception.

Sometimes, people determine their vision based on their personal attributes and privileges only. They later come under pressure when things don't work out as envisaged.

In Esther 6:6, the King asked Haman about who he thinks the king delights to honour, and he assumed it should be himself due to his personal attributes and privileges he has been enjoying in the palace. He later discovered that he was wrong, and his selfish thought then put him under pressure. In the end, he became manipulative and hated Mordecai and all the Jews. Haman later lost his life at the end.

Proverbs 31:30 says that favour is deceitful, and beauty is vain. This implies that personal attributes and privileges can deceive somebody into developing wrong ambition.

A brother came to me some years ago that he has oratory power with good communication skills. He then believed that he had been called to be a preacher. The man said he could really talk and speak to people. I then told him that talking is not enough to make him a preacher and that there are other skills he will need, including divine ordination.

Never develop a vision based on your personal attributes and privileges alone but consider other necessary factors. A vision based on personal attributes alone will bring pressure when it reaches a stage where it demands other skills you don't have.

5. The pressure of regret from a change of vision.

Sometimes, people replace one vision with another and later regret their action. This usually happens when they run into difficulty in their new vision. They start to think that maybe it would have been better for them to stay with their previous vision.

For example, a person that used to be an engineer and later changed his vision to be a teacher when he faced challenges in teaching, the person may start thinking that maybe it would have been better for him to remain in engineering. He may think that life would have been better for him if he were an engineer.

He will regret not being the person he was supposed to be. If this regret continues, this person may come under pressure to amend the error.

People usually look back into their former position whenever their new position gives them challenges. As a child of God, instead of putting yourself under the pressure of regret, try to see the big picture. It could be God that orchestrated your change of vision to protect and save your life from certain impending danger awaiting you in your former vision.

A brother told me some years ago that if he remained in his home country without relocating to a western country, he would have done well in life. I then told him that, *"What if God took you out to escape something sinister such as premature death?"* I told him that maybe he would have died if God did not take him out.

The reality of life is that there are challenges everywhere. Both your new and former vision will bring challenges on the way as you pursue them, but be ascertained that it is God leading you before you change direction as regards your visions.

Romans 8:28 (KJV): *"And we know that all things work together for good to them that love God, to them who are the called according to his purpose."*

The Bible verse above promises that all things, including good and bad, will work for your good. Therefore, instead of dwelling under the pressure of regret, believe the above promise from God's word and move on with your life. God can work all things out for your good in your new endeavour.

6. The pressure of your vision putting you in a position you don't like to be.

Vision will put you in the position you don't like to be in, but you must be ready to survive the pressure emanating from such a situation.

In 1 Corinthians 4:10, Paul wrote to the Corinthians that he and other disciples have become weak and fools for Christ's sake. Their pursuit of heavenly visions has made them become the persons they would not have liked to be, for nobody wants to be a fool or being despised.

In Colossians 1:24, Paul also stated that they rejoiced in their sufferings for Christ's sake. Their pursuit of heavenly visions put them in the position they would not have liked to be.

Furthermore, the same Paul revealed in Philippians 4:12 the secret of his survival when he found himself to be in the position he hated. He has learned how to be abased and abound. He has learnt how to survive and adapt to every situation he found himself in. This kind of skill removes the pressure that could come when he finds himself in the situation he hated. He knew how to fit into every situation, both good and bad.

As a person, I generally don't like to be in a position that presents me as a beggar. Some time ago, somebody promised our church some financial help for building work, and the person later became elusive. He chose not to pick my calls, then I chose to stop chasing him, but God told me not to be discouraged.

Amazingly, the person later fulfilled the promise. When your vision exposes you to situations you hate, deal with it with wisdom and patience. Do not be quick to abandon your vision because it is exposing you to situations you dislike.

7. The pressure from pursuing the right vision.

This is a pressure that comes when you are pursuing the right visions for your life.

This pressure comes through the price you must pay for the vision. There is always a price tag when you discover God's plan for your life. The price tags are things you will need to let go for you to pursue your vision.

In Genesis 12:4, Abraham departed from his country and his people that he was familiar with to be the person God created him to be. That was the price he must pay. Abraham must relocate to a place he was unfamiliar with and dwell among people he did not know before. What a price! It is evident that Abraham would have been under intense pressure to yield to the new vision God brought to him, but he had no choice but to obey.

Whenever you are chasing the right vision, there will always be pressure that you will need to overcome because there are things you must let go of so that your vision can stand.

A man of God was told by God that he was created to be a Pastor and a leader of a church. When the man received the message from the Lord, he came under intense pressure because to yield to that vision will force him to abandon the career he has built for many years. He yielded, and after many years, he had no regret of his decision. Every right vision will demand from you a price, and you must effectively handle the pressure that will come with payment of such price.

How can you overcome these pressures that visions bring?

1. Identify the sources of the pressure.
2. Pray against those sources to dry off.
3. If possible, walk away from the sources bringing pressure on you through your visions. For example, you can walk away from your past that is trying to disturb your present.
4. Create boundaries between yourself and the sources of pressure.
5. Choose not to take to heart every word thrown at you because sometimes, pressure comes through what people say. What God says matters than what men say.

6. Keep the right focus. Do not let pressure distract you from the right focus because whatever you focus on shall control your attention and action.

7. If it happens, accept rejection from the enemy of your vision. For example, those that are not ready to be part of your vision, let them go if they choose to walk away from you.

8. Put your trust in God. There are things you can control, and there are things you can't control. Entrust into the care of God those things you can't control, so that enemy will not be using things you can't control to oppress your mind.

9. Choose to think differently. When situations want to make you think negatively, decide to think in the opposite direction. For example, if the prevailing situation tells you that things will not work out well, tell yourself that things will work out well for you. Sometimes, the prevailing situation wants you to think contrary to the Bible but choose to think according to the Bible. Choose to think possibility.

10. Take a break. One of the ways to deal with pressure from vision is to know when to relax from what is putting pressure on you. This will help you to get fresh ideas during relaxation.

11. Distribute the pressure. Share your situations with somebody that can be of help. You may need to seek an able assistant to help with your visions and take some pressure off you.

12. Seek spiritual empowerment. Ask God to empower you so that you can overcome every kind of pressure coming upon you due to your vision.

Pray

- Father, let every arrow of frustration the enemy wants to throw at me backfire in Jesus' name.
- Father, whatever and whoever the devil has chosen to use to hinder my vision, let them fail in Jesus' name.
- Father, let every source the enemy uses to press me down dry off today in Jesus' name.
- Father, give me the grace to finish well and strong in every project I lay my hands on in Jesus' name.
- Father, you are the helper of the helpless. Help me to achieve success in all my visions in Jesus' name.

Chapter Nine

Turning vision into reality

It is one thing to have a vision, but it is another thing to turn that vision into a reality. To turn vision into reality means that you are bringing thoughts into physical existence. You are moving from I wish to I do. Until your vision comes into physical existence, it remains a wish. In this chapter, we want to explore how to bring vision into a reality.

To bring your vision into reality will require the following:

Write it down

Habakkuk 2:2 (KJV): *"And the Lord answered me, and said, write the vision, and make it plain upon tables, that he may run that readeth it."*

Do not just put your vision in your brain but write it down. What you have written down will always attract your attention as you can see it with your physical eyes where you had written it. This will help you to keep remembering your vision whenever you see where you had written it. A vision not written down will always escape your memory.

Simplify it

To simplify your vision means to break it down into different components for easy handling.

In Exodus 35:11-19, after Moses received a vision from God to build the tabernacle, he then broke it down into different component, what the construction work will require.

Many people get confused easily when things are muddled together but simplifying a vision will enable you to understand the work required to achieve the vision.

Gather the required information

Now that you have simplified your vision into different components, you need to start gathering information about handling each of the components. Such information may include where to obtain the materials, prices of every material, how to combine the materials for a better product, etc.

In Numbers 13:1-3, the Israelites sent spies to the land of Canaan to gather information that will enable them to take over the land. When you know what to do, you will be able to act rightly. Without relevant information, the plan will be destroyed. If you want your vision to succeed, avoid acting in ignorance.

Develop action plans

You will now need to develop action plans which will include details of works required for the vision to come into physical existence.

Luke 14:28-30 (KJV): *"For which of you, intending to build a tower, sitteth not down first, and counteth the cost, whether he have sufficient to finish it? lest haply, after he hath laid the foundation, and is not* *able to finish it, all that behold it begin to mock him, saying, this man began to build, and was not able to finish."*

In this verse, Jesus advised that we should not embark on any new projects without proper planning regarding works to be done.

Such a plan will include:

- Cost—how many resources you will need.
- Level of sacrifice needed. For example, how much of your time, sleep, or comfort will you sacrifice?
- Needed skills. When you develop a plan, you will be able to identify other must-have necessary skills and any other limitations you need to deal with. This will also help you to identify those who may have the skills you lack for your works.
- Steps to take. This will include daily, weekly, and monthly steps, etc. You should be able to draw a timetable of action detailing different steps you will take under different stages of the work.

Allocate time

It is unwise to have a vision with an indefinite time frame.

In Nehemiah 2:6, before the King, Nehemiah set the amount of time his work of rebuilding the walls of Jerusalem would take. It is important that you set the time you wish to achieve the plan and bring the vision into physical existence. This will give you a guide of time frame to work towards. Many people develop visions but without implementation because there was no set time for them. Though the set time may not be totally accurate, it will guide and help you detect time-wasting and unnecessary delay.

Take steps of faith

Pursuing your vision entails working under the unknown. You have no clue or details of how your situations will turn out to be as you get along with your vision. Pursuing a vision entails risk, and the only solution in dealing with risk is to be ready to act in faith.

What does it mean to take steps of faith?

It means to start with what you have.

It is impossible to have at the onset every resource you will need to complete your vision, but when you start with the little you have, God will then move into action to supply you with those things that you don't have. You will need to start with the little resources at your disposal while trusting God to supply the rest of the resources as you progress. Do not wait until you have all the required resources before starting your vision; otherwise, you may never start. As an act of faith, start with the little resources you have and keep thanking God for it and very soon, your act of faith will move God to multiply your little resources.

It means to start from where you are—your present location.

There is an adage: the journey of thousand steps will begin with one. Bringing your vision into a reality will require that you start taking steps from where you are, and you don't have to wait until you get into certain locations or positions. At the onset, you may not know in detail the direction to follow regarding your vision, but when you take the first step, God will take over the rest of your steps. Just do something to promote your vision, then you will see the door start opening for you to give you further direction.

Many people fall into deception, believing that they have not started their vision because they don't know where to start from, but the reality is that while you may not know where to start from, you can start from where you are at the moment. There is always something, though little, you can start with regarding your vision. For example, mere reading a small note about your vision can open your eyes to more things you can start chasing for your vision. God wants to order your steps, but you must take the first step; otherwise, there will be no step for God to order.

It means to start with what you know.

To bring your vision into reality will demand from you starting with what you know, and God will then start leading you and revealing to you what you don't know that you need to know. Do not wait until you know all things about your plans because it will never happen. There are new ideas to discover on the way as you progress with the journey. What you need to develop is to be teachable because as you progress along the journey of your vision, if you are teachable, you will come across new information that will add to your knowledge and aid your vision. Start with what you know about your vision, and you will discover more knowledge as you progress.

Isaiah 42:16 (KJV): *"And I will bring the blind by a way that they knew not; I will lead them in paths that they have not known: I will make darkness light before them, and crooked things straight. These things will I do unto them, and not forsake them."*

The Bible verse above boosts our faith that God will not leave us in darkness, but He will guide us out of darkness into light. Darkness could represent what you do not know. Unfortunately, there is always the unknown when it comes to vision, but when we trust God to guide us, we will have enough faith to start our vision despite elements of darkness around us. Never wait for the perfect condition before you start your vision because it will never happen.

Five factors that will determine the success

As you embark on turning your vision into a reality, you need to be aware of some basic factors that will determine the success of your vision.

a. Work factor

As you pursue your vision, you will need to identify from the onset the place of work which entails things you need to do and actions you need to take. Laziness will delay or frustrate vision. There is a time to work and a time to rest, but don't rest when you're supposed to work and don't work when you're supposed to rest. Otherwise, tiredness will mess up your plan. Many visions have failed because of laziness and too much rest.

b. Perseverance factor

Turning vision into reality will face many obstacles and challenges, but you must endure all the difficult situations. Sometimes, you will need to endure frustration, delays, opposition, fear, and attacks from the enemies of your vision, etc. Due to a lack of strong will, many people change their plan whenever they face difficulty. Challenges on the way of your vision do not indicate that your vision was a mistake, but it is a normal situation every good plan faces. Your vision will not be immune to challenges that come against a good plan. Instead of surrendering to challenges, derive motivation from them as evidence that you are on a good course. If you give up or change your plan whenever you face difficulty, you will not be able to achieve good plans in life. You can't keep on changing your mind whenever you face difficulty, but you must endure.

c. Thought factor

The law of attraction says likes attract likes. That is, good thought will attract good things and vice-versa. Thought has creative power. If you think evil about your vision, evil will be attracted to it, and if you think good about your vision, good will be attracted to it. Your thought pattern will affect your vision.

Furthermore, the way you think will determine your attitude, and this will determine your action. A negative thinking pattern will produce a negative attitude which will cause negative action. Therefore, be mindful of how you think, especially as different situations unfold. Be determined that no matter what happens as you pursue your vision, you will keep thinking good.

d. Wisdom factor

Wisdom is the application of knowledge. It is one thing to have the necessary knowledge for your vision, but it is another to be able to apply it accurately to your vision. It is God that gives wisdom and as you pursue your visions, always ask God for more wisdom.

e. Prayer factor

Prayer enables you to get heaven involved in your vision. You will soon discover that as you pursue your vision, many situations have a spiritual dimension. Pray before you start your vision; pray as you progress, and pray after you have completed it. Pray for yourself that you will have favour with men and that you will be contacted as you pursue your vision. Pray that you will have more than enough wisdom to pursue your vision and bring it to completion. Pray that God will help you to take good decision every time you pursue your vision. Pray for yourself to be stable and stay in faith irrespective of challenges on the way. As you pursue your vision, pray that the good hand of God will rest upon you so that you will never be weary or lack supply.

Similarly, pray against enemies of your vision. When you choose to pursue plans that will benefit your life and the people around you, forces of hell will set in motion a different kind of scheme to hinder your vision. However, through continual prayer, you will be able to defeat enemies of your vision.

Prayer

- Father, I thank you for every good thought you put in my heart.
- Father, from today, let your good hand be upon me and my vision in Jesus' name.
- Father, give me the wisdom to accomplish all my vision in Jesus' name.
- Father, overthrow every enemy of my vision and permanently silence every evil mouth speaking against it.
- Father, let all my visions speak to the glory of your name.

Chapter Ten

Psychological warfare

A visionary is a person who sees into the future. He has a plan of who he will become in future. Devil is always afraid of those who have visions because if they should succeed, they will set many people free from his bondage.

Therefore, Satan will employ diverse means to stop a man of vision. One of the methods Satan can use to stop the visionary is to use psychological warfare.

Psychological warfare is the use of actions intended to destroy the morale and wellbeing of a person. This is done by attacking the mind of the person using diverse intimidating strategies. In psychological warfare, the battlefield is the mind. Once the victim's mind is captured, his morale will become low, which may force the person to quit his vision.

In this chapter, we shall examine seven different methods Satan may use to intimidate your mind and destroy your morale regarding your visions.

1. Self-esteem

This is your confidence in your own worth or abilities. It is a sense of respect you have for yourself. Your self-esteem is the personal assurance you have about your competency and ability. It is impossible to succeed in a mission without a sense of personal competence. You need to believe that you have what it takes to succeed in your mission.

Satan always targets the self-esteem of people pursuing visions. He wants to convince them that they do not have what it takes to achieve their mission.

1 Samuel 17:33 (KJV): *"And Saul said to David, thou art not able to go against this Philistine to fight with him: for thou art but a youth, and he a man of war from his youth."*

In this verse, Satan spoke through Saul to bring down the self-esteem of David to convince him that he did not have what it takes to defeat Goliath. Similarly, in many situations, Satan could speak through the mouth of those around you to convince you that you lack the basic attributes required for your vision to succeed. When people around you start attacking your self-esteem to discourage you from pursuing your vision, you must know that the devil is at work against it.

Numbers 13:31 (KJV): *"But the men that went up with him said, we be not able to go up against the people; for they are stronger than we."*

In the above Bible verse, Satan attacked the self-esteem of Israelites such that they accepted that they did not have what it takes to defeat their enemies.

When you begin to think that you don't have what it takes to succeed in your vision, Satan is waging psychological warfare against your mind to destroy your morale.

1 Samuel 17:37 (KJV): *"David said moreover, the lord that delivered me out of the paw of the lion, and out of the paw of the bear, he will deliver me out of the hand of this philistine. And Saul said unto David, go, and the Lord be with thee."*

Instead of accepting the enemy's claim that he cannot defeat Goliath, David told Saul: *In God I put my trust.*

Your knowledge of what the word of God says about you will enable you not to yield and fall into the attacks of the enemy against your self-esteem.

2 Corinthians 3:5 (KJV): *"Not that we are sufficient of ourselves to think anything as of ourselves; but our sufficiency is of God."*

When an enemy attacks your self-esteem, you must always reply that your sufficiency is in the Lord, not your personal ability.

2. Character

As part of his psychological warfare strategies, Satan will also try to attack your character and personality to make you feel unworthy of God's help.

Satan will attempt to tell you that you are not a good person, and therefore, God will not help you achieve your mission.

1 Samuel 17:28 (KJV): *"And Eliab his eldest brother heard when he spake unto the men; and Eliab's anger was kindled against David, and he said, why camest thou down hither? And with whom hast thou left those few sheep in the wilderness? I know thy pride, and the naughtiness of thine heart; for thou art come down that thou mightest see the battle."*

In the above verse, Satan spoke through Eliab to attack the character of David to make him feel low. Eliab accused David of being a proud and evil person. He attacked his character. The scheme here is that Satan wanted David to see himself as a bad person that was not worthy of success. If David accepted that he was a proud and evil man, then Satan will progress to convince him further that the consequence of that was that God would not hear his prayer.

Be aware that whenever Satan speaks through somebody or reminds you of your fault, he is trying to lower your morale as regards your expectation and prayer for God's help. Satan likes launching psychological warfare against people to attack their mind and make them feel like an evil person unworthy of divine assistance, which they desperately need for their vision. When you need help from God, Satan will attack your mind and remind you of all your faults to destroy your confidence in God helping you. Satan always wants us to feel unqualified for divine assistance.

Therefore, when you start a vision, don't listen to the voice telling you that you are a bad person, and therefore, your plan will not succeed.

3. Foundation

This means your earthly generation and bloodline.

Satan will attempt to launch psychological warfare against your mind by attacking your foundation. For example, Satan will tell you that nobody in your bloodline has ever been successful in the vision you are trying to pursue. He will question your mind why you should be different from other members of your relation.

Judges 6:14-15 (KJV): *"And the Lord looked upon him, and said, go in this thy might, and thou shalt save Israel from the hand of the Midianites: have not I sent thee? And he said unto him, oh my Lord, wherewith shall I save Israel? behold, my family is poor in Manasseh, and I am the least in my father's house."*

In the Bible story above, when God called Gideon into his

ministry, Satan reminded him of his foundation that he came from a poor family. Satan's wiles reminded Gideon that his past betrays his future, and nothing at the beginning of his life guarantees his success in ministry.

Similarly, many people will not attempt a new idea because they believe that their upbringing did not equip them with the potential needed. Some of such people may even be afraid to be different from their relatives. They are not bold enough to be pioneers—the first in their family to achieve such a vision.

Therefore, if the devil attacks your mind, telling you that your vision can't succeed because of your background, reject his evil claims and suggestions.

4. Preparation

Satan can launch psychological warfare against your mind to stop your vision by attacking your preparation and experience. He will always try to convince you that you are not yet ready for your vision. He will query your experience.

Jeremiah 1:6 (KJV): *"Then said I, ah, Lord God! Behold, I cannot speak: for I am a child."*

When God also called Jeremiah into ministry, Satan reminded him that he was not yet of age. He peddled the thoughts that Jeremiah was not well prepared for it and has no experience for such an assignment.

The reason many are demotivated to start their vision is that they believe Satan's lies that they are not ready yet and that they still need to acquire some experience.

1 Timothy 4:12 (KJV): *"Let no man despise thy youth; but be thou an example of the believers, in word, in conversation, in charity, in spirit, in faith, in purity."*

Paul wrote a letter of encouragement to Timothy that he should not permit Satan to speak through people who may want to despise him because of his age. There are people that the devil will speak through to tell you that you have not yet acquired the necessary experience. When you face such intimidation, be bold and aspire to prove them wrong. Assure yourself that whatever idea God put in your mind, it is because you are ripe for it. While it is true that you may need a certain experience to pursue some visions, you can't wait indefinitely to acquire experience before you start your vision.

5. Faith

As part of his psychological warfare, Satan may launch an attack against your mind by questioning your faith in God. If you step out in faith, Satan will attempt to demoralise you by questioning your faith in God.

For example, he may raise technical questions that promote unbelief to destroy your faith.

Exodus 6:11-12 (KJV): *"Go in, speak unto Pharaoh king of Egypt, that he let the children of Israel go out of his land. And Moses spake before the Lord, saying, behold, the children of Israel have not hearkened unto me; how then shall Pharaoh hear me, who am of uncircumcised lips?"*

In these verses above, when God told Moses to go to Pharaoh again after the first failed attempt to receive a favourable response from Pharaoh, Moses put on a defence to resist God's instruction. Satan raised technical questions in the heart of Moses to discourage him from yielding willingly to God's instruction. Satan reminded Moses about his last failed attempt when he went to Pharaoh. Satan likes attacking our faith in God whenever we step out in faith.

If you have failed in a plan before and you want to try it again, Satan will remind you about your past failures and tell you that if your God can make you succeed, why did He not do it in the first attempt? He will ask you that what has changed now between your first failed attempt and the second attempt you want to make? He is trying to attack your faith in the Lord to make you quit.

This implies that you will need to be determined and strong in faith when choosing to step out in faith. Whatever the enemy throws at you to attack your faith in God, hold on to your faith, for your God will prove Himself in your situation. Refuse to draw back irrespective of what happens on the way.

6. Method

In his pursuit of psychological warfare against you to stop your vision, Satan will attempt to demoralise you by attacking your mind that your methods will not work. He will give you series of reasons why you must believe him that your method will fail.

1 Samuel 17:38-39 (KJV): *"And Saul armed David with his armour, and he put an helmet of brass upon his head; also he armed him with a coat of mail. And David girded his sword upon his armour, and he assayed to go; for he had not proved it. And David said unto Saul, I cannot go with these; for I have not proved them. And David put them off him."*

King Saul tried to convince David that he has no experience that could enable him to face and defeat Goliath in battle. When Saul could not prevail, he then gave David his armour. This implies that Saul was passing a message to David that whatever method or ammunition David might have would be inadequate to defeat Goliath, and therefore, his armour will be of great help.

Yet, David rejected Saul's offer passing a message that: *my method will work.*

Furthermore, in 1 Samuel 17:43, when Goliath saw the weapon David brought to fight him, he mocked David. At the end of the story, David defeated Goliath with his weapon once mocked by people.

Satan will always try to intimidate your strategy even if it were given to you by God. Therefore, do not surrender to that negative voice telling you that your methods and strategies will fail. When God gives you a method and strategy, it will work. Whatever method God gives you, it is the Spirit of God that will make it work, not your personal ability. When Satan tells you that your method will not work, remind him that it is not by power but by the Spirit of the Lord.

7. Work

In his pursuit of psychological warfare against you to stop your vision, Satan will attempt to ridicule and molest your work and what you are building.

This is to make you feel that you are not doing well.

Nehemiah 4:3 (KJV): *"Now Tobiah the ammonite was by him, and he said, even that which they build, if a fox go up, he shall even break down their stone wall."*

In the above story, when Satan could not stop Nehemiah from building the walls of Jerusalem, he started operating through human agents to ridicule his work by speaking ridicule through scoffers. Sometimes, enemies can come together to find fault in your work. They may start speaking negative comments about your work and despise it to discourage you, but you must be strong. If you keep your focus and keep going with your vision, the same people who mock your work will be permanently silent when you succeed. Let your success speak for you and do not answer mockers of your vision. The good news is that psychological warfare is winnable. To win a psychological warfare, renew your mind with God's word and do not listen to what people say but what the word of God says about you and your destiny.

In all situations, choose to think in the Kingdom way and refuse to think as the enemy wants you to think. Guide your mind and fill it with the word of God continually. When Satan put negative thought into your mind, refuse to think it.

Determine to see yourself as God sees you, not as the world sees you. Believe the identity the word of God says about you and reject every name human beings want to give you contrary to the word of God.

Whenever enemy launches a psychological warfare against your mind, think about the following Bible verse:

Philippians 4:8 (KJV): *"Finally, brethren, whatsoever things are true, whatsoever things are honest, whatsoever things are just, whatsoever things are pure, whatsoever things are lovely, whatsoever things are of good report; if there be any virtue, and if there be any praise, think on these things."*

Prayer

- Father, let every evil eye focusing on my life go blind from today in Jesus' name.

- Father, whoever and whatever enemy has arranged against my plan, overthrow them today in Jesus' name.

- Father, every tongue calling me a name you did not give me and speaking proud things against my plan, humble them and cut them off today in Jesus' name.

- Father, every psychological warfare arranged against my vision, let it collapse in Jesus' name.

- Father, concerning me and my vision, I declare: no more discouragement, demotivation, disappointment, mockery, fear, intimidation, inferiority complex, nervousness, in Jesus' name.

Chapter Eleven

The battles of a visionary

Vision is about who you are becoming in the future. That person you are becoming in the future will be far better and greater than the former. It is to the glory of God that you become a better and greater person. While God rejoices that you are becoming a better and greater person, the devil is not happy. Devil gets panic attacks whenever you develop a new vision that will make you a better and greater person. Therefore, to stop you from becoming this new person, the devil will throw many hindrances and obstacles on your way to stop your vision. Every successful visionary faced battles that wanted to stop them, and the success of their vision is evidence of their triumph over those battles. In many circumstances, the devil will personally attempt to stop your vision through his demons, and if he fails, he will use human agents. Due to the reality and inevitability of battles when you pursue a new vision, you must be aware of the different strategies the devil will explore to hinder your vision. In this chapter, we shall explore different means the devil will try to hinder your visions.

1 Thessalonians 2:18 (KJV): *"Wherefore we would have come unto you, even I Paul, once and again; but Satan hindered us."*

Satan hindered Paul from visiting the Thessalonians. This could be done in diverse means and at different stages of the vision.

Direct attack on stages of development of vision.

Anti-conception spirit

This is a spirit that hinders people from conceiving good ideas and vision. It creates a troubling environment that will disturb people's heart from thinking right and developing vision.

Every good idea begins with a thought. It is when the thought matured into fruitfulness that we can achieve our vision. The devil will always attack your mind from conceiving good ideas that will develop into vision. He will also always try to kill in your heart a good thought that has the potential of developing into a vision.

Proverbs 4:23 (KJV): *"Keep thy heart with all diligence; for out of it are the issues of life."*

To guard your heart will require that you mind how you think, and you should resist every attempt of the enemy to hinder the effectiveness of your heart. When the devil brings wrong thoughts into your heart, you must resist it. When he makes you think negatively, especially about your visions, you must resist it.

When the devil tries to keep your mind busy with troubles, you must be wise enough to detect that this is an attempt from hell to hinder you from thinking productively.

There are many good ideas the devil has killed from people's hearts through diverse attacks on their minds. Do not permit the devil to steal a good idea from your heart or hinder you from conceiving good ideas.

Incessant war and troubling engagement are clever ways the devil uses to hinder people from thinking good ideas. A person engulfed in series of troubles and problems will not have the time to think and develop a good idea.

2 Samuel 7:1-2 (KJV): *"And it came to pass, when the king sat in his house, and the LORD had given him rest round about from all his enemies; That the king said unto Nathan the prophet, See now, I dwell in an house of cedar, but the ark of God dwelleth within curtains."*

In the above Bible verses, it was when war ceased in the life of David that he thought to build a house for the Lord. Unless war ceases, it is difficult to conceive good ideas. Therefore, if you want to conceive good ideas, ensure that you maintain a peaceful atmosphere roundabout your life. Get rid of anything that will disturb your mind; otherwise, the enemy can kill good ideas and visions in your heart or hinder your heart from conceiving good ideas and visions.

Miscarriage spirit

This is a spirit that aborts good ideas and vision. It creates series of negative situations that will abort conceived vision. It is one thing to develop a good thought; it is another thing for the person to carry such thoughts safely to the stage of delivery. When the devil fails to hinder your mind from conceiving good ideas, he will attempt to cause a miscarriage of good ideas.

1 Thessalonians 2:18 (KJV): *"Wherefore we would have come unto you, even I Paul, once and again; but Satan hindered us."*

In the above Bible verses, Paul and his fellow disciples developed a thought to visit fellow workers in the ministry, but they could not bring the thought into action because Satan kept hindering them such that the thought eventually died out—it was never activated.

Whenever a good idea is developed in the heart, Satan will start throwing series of hindrances on the way to abort such good ideas.

Many times, the devil will use procrastination, excuses, and laziness to abort good ideas people conceived in the heart. Therefore, be mindful of whatever reasons causing you to delay action regarding your vision. When you notice that you are becoming too busy, such that you don't have enough time to pursue your vision, the devil is at work trying to abort your vision.

Anti-delivery spirit

This is a spirit that hinders the maturity of vision and safe delivery. Sometimes, people can conceive good ideas and carry them for many years, but when it is time to bring them into physical existence, the devil will strike with complications. There is a spirit that hinders the safe delivery of vision.

It is one thing to conceive a good idea and carry it in the heart for days, but it is another thing to deliver it safely into physical manifestation.

There are people that developed good ideas about a project, and they have done every necessary preparation, but when it comes to establishing the project, complications will stop them.

Why is it so difficult to deliver a conceived idea safely?

Isaiah 37:3 reveals that delivery requires strength. You need strength to push conceived ideas into delivery. Every pregnant woman that had delivered children will tell you that they must push at a certain stage for the baby to come out. Many people could not bring a good idea they have developed over the years into delivery because they seek a perfect condition before they can start transforming ideas into physical manifestation. They don't want to push themselves or inconvenience themselves. This is the devil's deception to delay or cancel the safe delivery of good ideas. Pushing will involve inconveniencing yourself, being ready to pay the price, fighting every contrary thing and struggling against every gravity that wants to pull you down. When the strength to push is greater than the force opposing delivery, we have a safe delivery. When you suddenly run out of strength to bring your long-conceived visions into physical manifestation, be aware that the devil is at work.

Spirit of infanticide

Infanticide is the killing of a person when young (an infant). It usually happens within the few days of existence. The spirit of infanticide also kills a young idea recently brought into physical manifestation.

It is usually tough to nurture a new project into its full maturity.

For example, when you start a church with few people or a business with very few customers patronising you, it will be challenging.

At the infancy stage, the enemy finds it easy to close a new project or organisation. The success of your vision scares the enemy, so he will try to kill it at the infancy stage.

Revelation 12:3-4 (KJV): *"And there appeared another wonder in heaven; and behold a great red dragon, having seven heads and ten horns, and seven crowns upon his heads. And his tail drew the third part of the stars of heaven, and did cast them to the earth: and the dragon stood before the woman which was ready to be delivered, for to devour her child as soon as it was born."*

In the above verses, the enemy attempted to kill a newly born child because of the fear of the future glory of the child. Therefore, when you bring alive a new vision, it is time to put in more effort to protect it against the spirit that kills newly born ideas. Ensure that you nurture your new vision very well. Newly established visions need protection and a safe environment to develop and thrive; otherwise, the enemy will kill it.

Anti-Growth spirit

This is a spirit that hinders the good and healthy development of vision.

Sometimes, a new project may not die, neither will it grow. Such vision experiences retardation and lack of development. When you notice that your new vision is not growing and remains stagnant for a long time, it may be because the enemy is at work. Devil is always afraid of big things because the bigger a thing becomes, the stronger it will be to resist attack.

Exodus 1:7-10 (KJV): *"And the children of Israel were fruitful, and increased abundantly, and multiplied, and waxed exceeding mighty; and the land was filled with them. Now there arose up a new king over Egypt, which knew not joseph. And he said unto his people, behold, the people of the children of Israel are more and mightier than we: come on, let us deal wisely with them; lest they multiply, and it come to pass, that, when there falleth out any war, they join also unto our enemies, and fight against us, and so get them up out of the land."*

In the above verses, King Pharaoh was afraid of the growth of the Israelites. He knew that there was strength in number. He then devises a means to make them small. Devil wants you to remain small so that he will find it easy to manipulate your destiny. When your project or vision is not growing, you will need to arise and explore the possible scheme the enemy may be using to keep your work small.

In Jeremiah 30:19, God promised to multiply you so that you will not be small. Growth is a divine agenda for whatever vision

God has given you. I pray for you that you shall not be small in Jesus' name.

Spirit of mockery

This is a spirit that raises people to mock your work to discourage you and probably stop your vision. When the enemy could not stop the work, he will start mocking it to discourage those doing it.

Nehemiah 4:3 (KJV): *"Now Tobiah the ammonite was by him, and he said, even that which they build, if a fox go up, he shall even break down their stone wall."*

When enemies could not stop Nehemiah from starting the rebuilding of the walls of Jerusalem, they started mocking the work.

Similarly, in your own private life, when you start a good idea, some people would have told you to stop it, but if you refuse and the work is making progress, they will start mocking the work. Some of these demon-possessed people can suddenly turn themselves into prophets of doom, prophesying evil concerning your work. All these attempts are from the devil trying to use mockery to stop your vision, but you must be strong. Never surrender to mockery. When your vision grows, all mockers will go silent. It is success that closes the mouth of mockers.

Gates of hell

This is a direct attack from the kingdom of darkness against good plans.

Matthew 16:18 (KJV): *"And I say also unto thee, that thou art Peter, and upon this rock I will build my church; and the gates of hell shall not prevail against it."*

Jesus promised that the gates of hell should not prevail against His church.

The word gates (plural) of hell means demonic attacks of different types.

It could be in the form of disunity among those assisting you in your vision, serious opposition from established authority, blackmailing from human agents, lack of financial resources, lack of customers to patronise your businesses, strife, accommodation problem, rejection, fault-finding from enemies, accusation and counter-accusation, etc.

When you notice problems coming from different directions against your plans, be aware that the devil is at work. When you notice the devil is at work against your plan, you need to handle the situation spiritually, not carnally.

Isaiah 59:19 (KJV): *"So shall they fear the name of the Lord from the west, and his glory from the rising of the sun. When the enemy shall come in like a flood, the spirit of the Lord shall lift up a standard against him."*

This Bible verse promises us divine intervention against demonic attacks and that when the enemy attacks us from a different direction, the Spirit of God shall rise against him. Therefore, if you notice gates of hell attacking your work, you can take solace in this word of God.

Prayer

- Father, let every flattering tongue, speaking proud things against my life, be cut off in Jesus' name.
- Father, let every work of Satan fashioned against my life fail in Jesus' name.
- Father, multiply me financially, spiritually, materially, and mentally. Make me grow and become a threat to my enemy in Jesus' name.
- Father, let whoever and whatever that wants to close what you had established through me be removed from my way in Jesus' name.
- Father, let every force that will not let me deliver all my good ideas safely be broken today in Jesus' name.
- Father, let every war and trouble hindering me from thinking and developing good ideas cease in my life today in Jesus' name.

Chapter Twelve

Enemies of visions

Every good idea will face challenges and opposition from both human agents and Satan. Your vision and dreams are not spared from such difficulties and opposition. Whatever and whoever comes against your vision is an enemy of your vision.

In this chapter, we shall examine some of the enemies of vision that may arise. This knowledge will enable you to spot opposition that frustrates your vision and how to deal with them. Vision fails because of the activities of the enemies of vision and due to the negligence on the part of the visionary.

Enemies of visions

Satan

In the last two chapters, we examined how Satan attacks different stages of vision and how he launches psychological warfare against the visionary in an attempt to stop their visions. Satan is an adversary of your vision, and he will try many things to stop your vision.

1 Thessalonians 2:18 (KJV): *"Wherefore we would have come unto you, even I Paul, once and again; but Satan hindered us."*

You need to know that any plan that will benefit you or other people will suffer attacks from Satan. Therefore, in your planning, don't forget to incorporate Satan's scheme.

How does Satan attack vision?

Satan attacks vision by creating series of hindrances. Examples of such hindrances are:

→ By influencing government.

If your vision is of great advantage to humanity, Satan can influence the government to create laws and policies capable of frustrating your vision.

In John 12:31, Jesus described Satan as the prince of this world. That is, Satan rules in the affairs of this world, especially if he is permitted to do so.

He has the capability to influence the government to create negative conditions that will hinder the destiny of the people.

In Daniel 6:1-10, when enemies of Daniel could not find any fault with him, they influenced the king to make a law that prohibits people from praying to any other god except the gods of the land.

Similarly, many nations act to create evil laws and decrees through Satan's motivation. Satan plans such evil laws and decrees to hinder the destinies of many innocent people living in such nations.

In Jeremiah 29:7, God told Israel to pray for the ungodly nation where they lived; otherwise, that nation's government will make laws and policies that will hinder their comfort.

Therefore, if you notice that the government of the nation where you dwell suddenly starts making laws and decrees that seem to target your plan, it could be that Satan is at work by operating through the government of the land to hinder your vision.

→ **By influencing the community negatively.**

Satan can negatively influence the tradition, belief, opinions, and perception of the community members.

For example, Satan can make people have a perverted view of certain people and certain things.

In John 1:46, Nathanael said that any good thing could not come out of Nazareth. This represents a perverted view of people from such a community.

Similarly, Satan can influence a certain ethnic section of the society to believe that people from certain ethnic background are not good in certain activities and businesses. It implies that people may not patronise projects or businesses established by people who hail from such ethnic backgrounds with the stigma of incompetence.

When you notice that your vision does not enjoy public acceptance, which is desperately needed in order to thrive, it could be that Satan has given those people negative perception about your community.

→ **By entering people and stirring up hatred and attack.**

Satan can create enemies and influence one community against the other.

In Luke 22:3, it is written that Satan entered Judas to influence him to rise against Jesus.

When you notice hatred from people regarding your vision, it could be that Satan is influencing them against you because of it.

→ **By causing wastage.**

The Book of Isaiah 54:16 describes Satan as a waster who goes around to cause destruction.

If given opportunities, Satan can waste resources, time, energy, opportunities, etc.

Therefore, be clever and urgent to close every door that Satan can exploit to cause wastages. Think carefully before you invest huge resources into your new vision that you had not tested. To guide against the possibility of waste, gradually introduce resources into your vision and monitor how situations are evolving. Be prudent.

→ **By causing diverse difficulties that will bring delays.**

When you notice strange situations affecting your vision, it could be a sign that Satan is at work against your vision. Sometimes, Satan can keep you busy with irrelevancies to distract you from the right focus or bring you into confusion such that you get disorganised and mess up the work. Be careful and vigilant.

Self

If you don't put yourself under strict control, you can become an enemy of your own vision. Therefore, it is important that you put yourself under adequate and constant examination and control so that you don't destroy your own vision.

How can you destroy your own visions?

→ **Lack of revelational knowledge.**

Habakkuk 2:3 (KJV): *"For the vision is yet for an appointed time, but at the end it shall speak, and not lie: though it tarry, wait for it; because it will surely come, it will not tarry."*

According to this verse, vision is for an appointed time—time of its full fulfilment. If your vision is from God, you should find out about the set time for your visions. If you lack understanding of the set time God has for your visions, you may end up messing things up either by being too slow or fast.

In order not to miss God's timing for your vision, don't be too slow or fast. Be patient and let situations unfold themselves naturally in accordance with God's timetable. Avoid being too pushy or manipulative.

→ **Character problems.**

Your bad character will hinder you from relating very well with destiny helpers that God sent to help you fulfil your vision.

Therefore, Proverbs 18:24 advises that a man that hath friends must shew himself friendly. You will not be able to attract helpers of destiny if you have an unfriendly attitude. If you notice that nobody wants to help you, check your character; maybe you are not a friendly person.

→ **Lack of wise counsel.**

Proverbs 24:6 (KJV): *"For by wise counsel thou shalt make thy war: and in multitude of counsellors there is safety."*

There are visions you can't achieve alone because you need credible advisers to put you through. If you have no one to learn from and yet you don't have all the relevant knowledge, your visions may fail. When you don't know what to do, seek those who are more knowledgeable than you for proper counsel.

→ **Poor foundation.**

Many visions fail because of a lack of proper foundation and preparation.

Luke 14:28 (KJV): *"For which of you, intending to build a tower, sitteth not down first, and counteth the cost, whether he have sufficient to finish it?"*

Proverbs 24:27 (KJV): *"Prepare thy work without, and make it fit for thyself in the field; and afterwards build thine house."*

The two Bible verses above emphasize the importance of proper preparation before starting a vision.

Evidence of poor foundation include:

- lack of adequate preparation,
- lack of relevant knowledge about the visions,
- lack of planning,
- lack of direction,
- lack of knowledge about where to obtain resources from,
- lack of strategies and methods to apply,
- lack of timetable to follow, etc.

When you suffer from the above, it may lead to the collapse of your vision. Do your homework thoroughly before you start your vision.

→ **Laziness.**

Laziness means being unwilling to work. If you are lazy, you will become an enemy of your vision.

Though you may not agree that you are lazy, the evidence of laziness includes:

→ **Procrastination—always delaying action.**

A lazy man will always say I will do it next time, but when next time comes, he will say another next time until he did nothing about it.

It is wise for you to understand that procrastination is an enemy of grace. When you delay acting at the time of grace, the door of grace will be closed, and doing it next time will be difficult.

→ **Talking without action.**

A lazy man only talks but no action. You cannot build a castle by only talking. Every good idea requires relevant action to bring it into physical manifestation. Do not only talk but do it.

→ **Doubt**

Doubt is a feeling of uncertainty and lack of conviction that makes you see impossibility. Doubt is a spirit, and it can include self-doubt (a situation when you have no confidence in yourself), doubting God (a lack of trust in God that He will help you), and doubting people (this is when you don't believe that people will come to help you in your vision). When you begin to have anxiety and doubt, deal with your faith level.

Human beings.

Another enemy of vision is human beings. Fellow human beings can hate your vision for various factors that can be linked to envy.

Proverbs 27:4 (KJV): *"Wrath is cruel, and anger is outrageous; but who is able to stand before envy?"*

The above Bible verse establishes that man rises against another man's plan, usually due to envy. Envy is to be angry at a man due to his achievement or success.

Ecclesiastes 4:4 (KJV): *"Again, I considered all travail, and every right work, that for this a man is envied of his neighbour. This is also vanity and vexation of spirit."*

Based on the above verses, you must be aware of three types of neighbours that can hate you out of envy due to your visions. Let's see them:

Close associates and friends

There are some close associates of yours who will become angry towards you out of envy when they hear about your vision. People that are not busy with their own vision will have time to hate you due to your vision. That is why you need to keep certain visions of yours secret and let it develop before you begin to tell people; otherwise, you may suffer attacks even before you start the vision.

Observers

These are people that are not connected with you, but they see your vision moving on. Similarly, due to envy, they may rise against it.

When such people see you succeed, they get motivated by envy and start to work against your vision.

To avoid such attacks, it may be important for you to cover your vision until it is fully matured.

Household enemies

These are your relatives.

In Genesis 37:11, it was Joseph's brothers that sold him to slavery due to envy. They envied his dream. People of your house are the most easily accessible people the devil can use to attack you because they have better information about you than outsiders.

It is, therefore, advisable that before you share your vision with anybody, think carefully about it and have conviction in your heart before you do it.

How to deal with enemies of your visions.

- Examine yourself and deal with your weaknesses.
- Press on. Be ready to fight every hindrance that comes your way. Never quit.
- Set a watch. Set a watch against the enemy of your vision. Be at alert to detect the scheme and wiles of the enemy. Do not be careless.
- Be confident in God that He will finish what He started in your life.
- Pray without ceasing. Pray always. Pray before you start your vision. Pray as your vision progresses; pray till you finish your vision and pray after you had finished your vision.

Prayer

- Every evil agent hired against my visions, Father, remove them from my ways today in Jesus' name.
- Father, strengthen my hands, mind, heart, and spirit in all my purpose in Jesus' name.
- Father, favour that overrules any opposition or obstacles, release it on me today in Jesus' name.
- Father, whatever dwells inside of me, capable of frustrating my destiny, let it die out of me today in Jesus' name.
- Father, make my vision speak in Jesus' name.

BOOKS FROM THE SAME AUTHOR

Journey to the Next Level

The New Creature

Building a Glorious Home:
A Pathway to a Successful Marriage

Enemy of Marriage

Words That Heal

The Winning Formula

Faith That Always Wins

Common Mistakes Parents Make About Their Children

Recovery is Possible

When You Are Desperate For A Miracle

Decision Making
Explore a Path to Godly Decision Making

Stop your fear before it stops you

This book, and all these other books from the same author, are available at Christian bookstores and distributors worldwide.

They can also be obtained through online retail partners such as Amazon or by contacting the author at the address below:

21-23 Stokes Croft, Bristol. BS1 3PY. United Kingdom

Email: info@fkasali.com | Website: www.fkasali.com

Telephone: +44 (0) 77271 59 581